Instructions To Money

From Welfare To Millionaire

By: Daniel W. Merrick, Ph.D.

ISBN 145373774X   **EAN-13** 9781453737743

To Robert & Laura
You made me believe.
I wish you could have seen this.

"The only way to surely fail; is never really try"

ABOUT THE AUTHOR

Captain Daniel W. Merrick, Ph.D., was born in the late 1950's and grew up on the lower east side of Cleveland, Ohio. While attending Collinwood High School he completed two years credit in Bible college education and graduated with his high school diploma in only three years. He went on to attend Chicago Bible College, Cleveland State University, Nashville School of Broadcasting, John Carroll University, University of Louisville, University of Kentucky, and The Hebrew Institute for Yahudime Biblical Studies.

Captain Merrick enlisted in the Army in 1979 and moved up in the ranks to Staff Sergeant before completing Officers training. He was commissioned a Second Lieutenant in 1982 and attended Armor Officers Basic and Armored Cavalry Advanced courses at Fort Knox Kentucky. Captain Merrick suffered a service-related disability and moved into civilian life where he became a salesman and radio announcer for worldwide broadcast of "Faith in Action" with the Ken Gaub Evangelistic Association.

In 1992, forced into the public welfare system by his service-related disability, Captain Merrick did not give up even in the face of insurmountable odds. In 1993 he released an album of musical works, which he wrote entitled 'Aliyah'. Daniel received the ASCAP popular music award in the Christian Music category in 1994 through 1998 for his work as a songwriter. In 1999 he completed a Yahudime translation of the Bible. In 1999 his family history and genealogy paper was completed entitled "The History and Genealogy of Merrick". That same year along with his father and wife, Daniel started RDJ Catalog.Com where he presently is the Corporate President.

Daniel (Daniyah, his Hebrew name) is a messianic Jew from the tribe of Levi and has appeared on several Christian Television programs such as Cornerstone Televisions "His Place" and "Getting Together". Read how Captain Merrick and his wife overcame the tide against them to grow from welfare to Millionaire in just seven years using 14 rules and a positive attitude that have made men wealthy in America for over 100 years.

CONTENTS

Always a borrower and a lender be

This old cliché was repeated with revolting repetition over the coffee tables of the poor and nameless when I was a boy: "Never a borrower or a lender be". Yet all those heard reciting this mantra had nothing, were in debt, and had no hope of ever rising above the class amenities that come with big deals and large credit lines. My first rule, although contrary to the old cliché', has a caution with it.

Most people use this saying to mean that if you borrow or lend more than you can afford that you will get into trouble. But that ideology came before the phrase Other Peoples Money or OPM. It's not just a movie, OPM is how banks and investors get rich and prosper. OPM makes movies, CD's, builds businesses, and can be a tool to help you gain the goals and dreams you want in life.

However, if you were borrowing to get deeper in debt for the purposes of buying things that do not produce an income, then this old meaning would apply. I am talking about borrowing to gain income producing gains, and lending, "Other People's Money", to create short-term gains. To do this, you must start with a goal and objective list, a product, a mentor, and resource lenders.

Let us start with Mentor(s). This is the first part of true wealth building. When working as a consultant for sales companies in the past, I discovered a three-step plan that works every time. You cannot learn how to be successful from someone who is not. Most Americans are taught to get a good education, get a job, and work for someone else making them rich. So we go to high school, then college, and then we get in debt.

J.O.B. equates to Jackass of Boss, or Just Over Broke, and the final equation of hourly slavery with too much of the month left at the end of the money. I take no credit for this acronym, J.O.B., which has been proven to be true by countless millions who work every day for someone else. Teachers give a great contribution to the country's wealth of knowledge in America. Although, if you ask an

4

economics professor how to be a millionaire, they would be lacking the real answer, because *they are not millionaires.* It is just that simple. Now we can see that the only way to know how to be a millionaire is to find one who can show you how. When I was on welfare I talked to others on welfare, and they told me how to work the system and stay on welfare. To make fifty thousand dollars a year, I would need to find a man who incomes $50,000 a year and learn from him how he did it. So if I truly want to be a millionaire, I need a millionaire to show me how.

The answer here is just to **meet**, **learn**, and **duplicate**. If you want to be a Millionaire selling Kirby Vacuum Systems then meet a Kirby Millionaire, learn what he or she did to get there, and duplicate it. Carnegie writes of this key to success in his books. Many others have used this method to gain great material success in America. Everything from Amway to KFC has used this duplication method to grow and prosper businesses worldwide, and so can you.

Throughout this book you will find that I have used various ideas and methods to outline how I succeeded and became a millionaire. Before we go any further, I want to let the reader know that there are no monopolies on good ideas. I credit the mentors I followed as having first plowing the path that I have taken. In turn, I have enveloped their ideas and put them into my own words formulating my story. I hope to put a new light on the subject and give a solid plan to my readers here. I thank you, the reader, for choosing me as a mentor in part by buying this book.

I personally selected as my mentors such people as Zig Ziglar, Tom Hopkins, Dale Carnegie, Napoleon Hill, Carlton Sheets, Ken Guab, Robert Kiyosaki, and a friend by the name of Mel. I cannot stress enough the importance of reading good material and using that resource as a base of knowledge to grow and understand the road map to wealth. Books such as "Think and Grow Rich", "How To Master The Art of Selling", "Re-arranging Your Mental Furniture", "Secrets Of Closing The Sale", "Rich Dad, Poor Dad", "The Magic of Thinking Big", and "How To Win Friends and Influence People" line my book shelf as an ever present mentor group that lends ideas and advise at a glance.

Another ideal way to get a mentor is through home study courses. We all have seen the late night TV infomercials and many scoff at the courses and the promises of great wealth. We all read the small print and see the disclaimer, "your results may very" at the end of the promotion. Some of these courses do have very good information compiled into readily accessible bundles for easy reference. Among these courses; Carlton Sheets' "No Down Payment" course is backed by documented success and his personal experience as a Real Estate Broker and Investor. One of the real advantages to these courses is that you have audio and video instructions and encouragement that can assist you if your spirits get low.

Maintaining a positive attitude is very important on the way to gaining wealth. The only way to surly fail is to never really try or give up before you reach the goal. I have read personal biographies of countless founders of successful ventures who while trying went bankrupt, failed, suffered divorce, losses of family and friends, and were ridiculed as crazy in the public eye. When eggs get broken the best way to make an omelet is to have a cheering section on your side. When the runner falls, gets up and dusts off the dirt, and keeps in the race that is the person who will finish the course. Others may finish before, but I am going all the way. That is the attitude of a winner who will be a success by using their unique talent to bring a new way of thinking about problems with new solutions.

Finding a personal mentor is important and can help you finish the race. You may not know someone who can stand in for you on a one on one advice session. That is where materials such as those I have listed above can get you started.

In 1995 I was living in a three-bedroom trailer and living on $583.00 a month salary. My wife and I were hard pressed to make ends meet and that is when I sought a way out of my poverty condition. I came across a program that helped me begin by buying my home with no money down and stating our own business. We had no money to begin with so the only recourse left was to use other people's money.

I found a product that my wife could sell door to door and I could drive and help her close the deal. The next step was to find a finance company that would loan money against the product and not hold us responsible for default if the customer didn't pay. We were able to do this with some help from persons who I sought out that knew of several companies that loaned for such direct sales programs.

You must remember that we were hungry. That was a motivating factor that could not be ignored. When your child needs food you find any way possible to make things happen and feed your child. That is where my wife and I came from and with bad credit to boot.

Kirby, Filter Queen, Rainbow, and countless other companies such as Cutco have programs that can give you a means to be a direct sales professional and help you develop an unlimited income. All you have to do is be teachable and learn. If you are where I was then and need a list of possible products to begin your own real business that will pay the bills, if you are faithful and work every day, you may email us at rdjcatalog.com and we have a program that can help you get started. I started by borrowing $2000.00, which I used to get door opening gifts and products to sell with financing in place. I paid back the money with sales proceeds and started our company RDJ Catalog.Com

I took what I learned with other direct sales companies and started with a plan and goal work sheet. My wife and I took the profit on each item sold and came up with a plan on how many presentations of our product we had to show a week based on the number of shows needed to make one sale. Then we reviewed our credit report and made a plan to remove our bad credit by paying off bad debts with the profits from our company's sales. Within two years we had an excellent credit rating and had laid the groundwork for an OPM expansion of our income.

We then selected several investments that would build our net worth. We purposefully avoided stocks due to the high risk involved with traditional Wall Street investments. The income production of our business along with income form our choice of residential real estate rentals, made for a ideal blend to build on for

7

upward economic growth. We also used collectable coins and gems, which we purchased, from the wholesale market.

You must remember that I cannot work. My condition prevents me from great physical labor so the effort here was to center on passive secure income that will be maintained with little or no effort. So real estate seemed to be one of the best methods. Another good method we used with our real estate today is coin operated laundry and vending machines at our properties. These provide good short-term income during the milk money crunch between rents and sales of other products from our catalogs.

So let me recap with a short list, what we did to get started:

Review options.
Wrote a plan with goals.
Chose mentoring programs and people.
Chose a product.
Started a Direct Sales Company.
Found loan companies to give credit to our customers without recourse.
Sold our products door to door.
Reviewed our credit rating and used profits to payoff bad debts and improve our credit rating.
Improved our net worth with collectables and real estate.
Improved our real estate with passive income resources such as vending machines.
Developed new goals, ideas, products, and services and started the cycle over.

Here is the formula I used when borrowing money for myself:

B=Amount Borrowed
I= Income from purchase using borrowed money (monthly)
T=Time
P=Profit (monthly)
C=Cost
R=Reinvestment
Y=Yield

For example I needed to Borrow $2000.00 to get started. I knew that I would have to pay it off quickly or get eaten alive with interest. So I first found out that my payment would be $40.00 from the credit card bill monthly. With the two thousand I bought 5 sets of cookware and all the forms and gifts I needed to get started. The cookware gross was $5000.00 when sold at a thousand dollars a set.

B=$2000   I=$5000 T=one month P=$3000 C=$2000
R=$2000 Y=$1000

Since we sold the five sets of cookware and made $1000 for our bills after paying off the credit card, we were still ahead by replacing the original investment in R= Reinvestment. The next step was to shorten the time and move toward a monthly 'Y' equal to about $4000 to $5000. This is easily done without hiring anyone as long as you're willing to work hard.

Remember that borrowing money for making money should be short term and result in a replacement of the investment at least 200% so you can remain in business for the next time period. Start out with a month since all bills are on a monthly basis, and you can better manage money the way that society has already planned. Plan to pay off the original debt within a month or two. Once you have a few months of sales under your belt then you are ready to start a borrowing plan that will make income with real estate and other items for a longer term. Using BIT-P-CRY helps us to understand what we need to do to make money on a short term while avoiding large risks. You don't need to cry when you BIT-P-CRY.

It is important to start with a product that sells for a thousand dollars or more to insure a good profit. The reality is that we all work in some way in sales. Most people produce or sell a product, good, or service. Even the act of getting a job is selling yourself and the service you will provide as an employee to an employer. The bottom line here is that millionaires don't work for others they work for themselves.
Goals are the foundation and road map to get where you want to go. Using Loan Companies to lend money to others makes you a lender.

Borrowing using the method I have used above, and actually did, shows a way to overcome the first steps of business without having to sell the family heirlooms. By duplicating this method with selling houses or land or businesses and commercial property one can use this rule properly and apply it to gain great wealth.

If you do not have a lending resource to get your start up capital, then you can save the money over a short period of time using recycling or a garage sale to raise the funds to get started. My wife and I saved the money from deposits on soft drink cans and had garage sales many times to raise funds for investing.

Remember to always use OPM and lend their money generously when selling your goods. Never borrow more that you can pay off in less than three months for short-term direct sales business. Trump Towers were built on OPM and banks lend with interest every day of the week. Whether you are going to use something like Cutco knives or my Cookware, it has little difference as long as you do your homework and do it for yourself and your family.

By the way, if you expect to own a million dollars worth of property and businesses, you're going to have to borrow money somewhere along the way. The prospects of saving that much before you are too old to enjoy it are just about assured. Most people in America will earn close to a million dollars stretched over 40 to 50 years. So if you want to speed up the process you're going to have to use this rule.

Fear will not get you out of the situation you are in. You must go forward into a planned battleground of getting bankers and loan companies to work with you. Writing a business plan can help also when it comes to starting your own business. Many local colleges or the SBA has many resources to help you get started. There are also government-backed programs that can help you start a business. Local resources such as the chamber of commerce will have a resource list of programs and agencies that can help. All that is required is the willingness to ask for help. Go down to your library and you can get several books on how to write a business plan. In today's world of Internet connectivity all you really need is a computer and go to SBA.GOV

Before I end this chapter it is important to me that you understand that my tactics may go against the tide of modern Christian thinking. Many finance gurus are out there telling everyone to pay off their bills and hunker down for the big asteroid or some catastrophe to hit the earth. I do believe in being debt free, still most people do not have the means to be debt free when it comes to buying a car or house. Therefore, I take a more realistic approach in using debt to build wealth and buy income greater than debt. Eventually with enough monthly cash yielding investments you gain enough to pay off debt and secure your future investments also. Later in this book I will reveal a little known secret that banks and governments use to apply this rule and never make a payment on the debt. But for now, it is best that we take this in a progressive way so that your mind is ready to understand it. So lets look at some little known facts that may lay out where most people are in the grand scheme of financial life in America. Here are some real facts that you may not know.

The average American works half a year to pay for their taxes.

The average American works for 40 years and retires on less than $1ooo a month.

The average American earns a million dollars over 40 plus years.

Most people don't even get a gold watch when they retire.

Most people are taught to work hard and bring home a living.

Indentured servitude was outlawed in America over 150 years ago.

Most Americans work for less than they can afford to live or retire on
Letting someone else tell them what their worth.

Most Americans will die before collecting one half of what they pay in Social Security.

Only one out of 40,000 people will ever make a living in some multi-level marketing program.

Over 80% of the self-made millionaires in the last 25 years did it in business for themselves.

Every business in the world sells a product or a service. Everybody buys products and services that they need.

Most Americans work for someone else who they have never met making that person rich.

Maybe it is time to start owning the means of production instead of letting the means of production own you. During our venture starting out, we worked with distributors of other products such as Kirby. If you are not able to get the money at hand to start, let Kirby or another direct sales organization help you get started by training you how to sell direct to the customer at home. Our company RDJ Catalog has a great opportunity to help you get started with our cookware, Vortech Force vacuums, or just selling out of our catalog. You can email me at Daniel@rdjcatalog.com and include your address and we will send some information to you about our programs.

The important thing to remember is how much you are worth. The average American will earn one million dollars or more in a lifetime of work. Since you are already a million-heir, why not learn how to accelerate your potential and achieve multi-millions?

To summarize, borrowing small amounts of money wisely to begin a direct sales business is an acceptable risk when used for the intended purpose of starting wealth acquisition. There is no law against borrowing good ideas either. Use good ideas that others have been successful with to implement your plan and achieve your dreams and goals while finding lending sources to provide product financing to your customers.

Helping your customers to fit financing of your products into their budget can start you on the road to great wealth and a customer base to build your business. Remember that nothing moves off the shelf and no money changes hands in America or the world for that matter unless someone sells it to those who need it. No matter what the product or service you choose, success is found in finding the need of your customer and filling that need with your product or service. One of my favorite writers and public speaker on these sales methods of finding the need and filling it is Zig Ziglar. In his books on sales and sales techniques, he shows how to present products of high quality like the cookware that we carry, to customers and save them money over a lifetime. By supplying customers with warranties and superior products, it helps them to own their products throughout their lives and pass them on to their grandchildren. 'Sales' is a learned profession Zig says: "like a Doctor or a Lawyer, the professional salesperson learns how to provide the customers with quality products and services".

I suggest that you purchase some of his books and learn how to sell before attempting to start any business you may choose. Many sales companies provide free training to their representatives and you may best find your start in a company such as the ones I mention in this book. Perhaps borrowing their resources already in place, will give you a network of allies to begin your road to multi-millions, being that we already know that you are a millionaire even if you do nothing but work for a living in America.

To close this chapter I will share with you the formula that I have used in many sales training sessions that show how easy it is to become a million dollar earner using direct sales.

Take a product like the Kirby Vacuum or Cookware that sells for $1000.00 or more as an example. If you sell that product for $1000 and you make an average of $400 profit after all your costs what would it take to make one million in profit after say two years?

To start this venture you will not be able to do it alone. First of all you would need to sell 105 units a month to do it alone and that would mean 4 a day with no time off for rest. But what if you got 9 people to help you achieve that and paid each one $100 a sale. Then you could easily achieve your goal and help others to make some extra money part time.

Dan with Kirby President Frank Venditti

The math is simple: 10 people including you doing 11 to 15 sales a month. I suggest 15 as a goal since that is what Kirby uses and many other companies have used that as an achievable goal.

$10 \times 15 = 150 \times 400$ (profit) $= \$60,000 \times 12$ months $= \$720,000 \times 2$ (years) $= \$1,440,000.00$ after taxes and write offs with a good accountant paying your taxes correctly you should be around a million. I will show you a similar breakdown in the next chapter that will deal with more accurate figures to show how you can easily earn a million in 2 to 4 years

If you are willing you can do anything. One of the dumbest people I ever knew was a multi-millionaire. He had little common sense also. But when it came to deals in Real Estate, he was sharp as a tack. He had not graduated from elementary school. Yet he knew how to get others to help him. If you learn how to win over helpers on the way to your goal, you will learn an immensely valuable skill.

How much you have in your pocket is not determined by your education, but by your willingness to learn and your determination.

14

I don't think Trump was right about being born a, "deal-maker", it must be learned. Anyone with the desire to learn it will succeed if they keep trying. Even if you are not a "deal-maker" and totally untalented, for the right price you can hire someone to help you do it. Winning friends and influence are not always easy to do, but they can be done if you create the right buzz around your project. In the entertainment industry they call it buzz. The art of creating interest in a recording or album coming out before it hits the shelves. Movie producers do it also. Get the marketing going by word of mouth before they ever get started making the film.

Pre-release glitz and dazzle painted with words traveling in the strongest network in the world, (rumor control and rumor central we called it in the Army) Create positive excitement around you that will get people interested in what you are doing.

When you borrow, borrow some of this good well and buzz and you may find that your project gets off the ground a little easier.

Sale at a profit of 300% mark up

You walk into the store and the sign reads '30% off sale' and you think 'what a bargain'. The reality is that the item you purchase at retail price reflects a wholesale cost, manufacturing cost, and markup costs that include labor, light bills, water, heat, air conditioning, taxes, and other costs of operations. The real costs are manufacturing, materials, and shipping. Even after these costs with the wholesalers profit, the cost to the retailer is about one third of the price when it is on sale. In other words, a 300% to 3000% markup for that skirt your daughter buys.

So once we know that we are paying $20 for the skirt that cost the store $1.80 there is little room for wonder on why the rich get richer. So why cry about it? In fact most businesses have such overall large overhead that if they did not sell at 300% or better they would go out of business. The cost of electric, labor, taxes, heating and air conditioning, and supplies such as paper and pens, brings the mark up cost of goods sold to a much higher level.

Last year my wife bought a 121 Karat emerald. It was appraised for $58,000.00 and the cost was substantially less than the appraised value. If she sold it at an auction house she might get $40,000.00 for the stone. At Tiffanies' that same stone might sell in a mounting for upwards of $2,000,000.00. The real difference here is the value received rather than the value. With the value comes the status of where the item was purchased.

Value building tools for the direct salesperson are based on quality, reliability, and cost savings over a lifetime of enjoying the benefits of ownership. Hence Ford verses Rolls Royce is distinguished not just in name, but also in service and warranty. That is why I choose cookware for my product to begin my business.

For years on and off I had worked for other direct distributors of products and found that there was an element of razzle-dazzle in the presentation of the product. Good showmanship is a part of any product from packaging to advertising. The best way to market at a 300% or better mark-up is to have superior quality that will last a lifetime. Let's take a look at the numbers on retail $1000.00 set of lifetime warranty cookware like the one we sell on our web site. Below we will break down the cost of goods sold and show our mark-up. From that information we can structure or goals.

Cost of Goods Sold	$300.00
Finance Costs	$100.00
Shipping	$ 40.00
Travel	$ 10.00
Forms & Paperwork	$ 1.90
Phone	$ 3.90
Gifts at the door	$ 5.00
Total	$460.80
Net Profit	$539.20

Now lets say that we want to pay off a credit card this month that has a $5000.00 balance. In addition our bills and living expenses are $900.00 for the month. Now the national average for sales in all fields is 3:1

That means that we have to show our product 3 times to get one sale. Now we need $5,900.00 to meet our stated goal here.

$5,900 ÷ $539 = 10.946 or 11 sales to reach our stated goal. If we need to show the product 3 times to make one sale then we need to show it 33 times to make 11 sales. If you work a 5 day work week then you will have 20 days to show the product 33 times. 33 ÷ 20 = 1.65 or two times a day. The product I choose, cookware, has a demonstration time of about one hour including paperwork. That is a 40-hour work month not including driving time to and from my chosen work area. Now if our goals prove out, and they have for me over and over by just doing what I have learned from those who showed me how to do this, we will earn 11 X $539.20 for the month and ÷ that by our 40 hours we come up with our wage working in business for ourselves of +-about $150 per hour. Now if you are like me and have a disability you can still work for two weeks and take two weeks off if you are willing to show your product four times a day. If you are really totally disabled you can hire some one

17

else to show the product, pay him or her $100 a sale, and make $439.20 per hour doing very little.

Now if you had ten people working for you showing your product and they made 11 sales each a month or a total of 110 sales a month then you would make $48,000.00 a month doing very little. But for forty-eight grand a month I bet you could look busy. Now before I get you too excited let me show you what our home based business will generate with little overhead and ten people working part time for us for one year.

Five hundred and seventy nine thousand, seven hundred and forty four dollars US cash $579,744.00.
So you may ask why isn't everybody doing it? I don't have a clue why; I just know that I am. Why aren't you?

Along with this rule goes the added value of buying at wholesale to market at retail. If you need a good dependable product line our company will be glad to offer you distribution and training to help you get started. RDJ Catalog also has finance plans to help fit your needs and provide customer loan programs.

Now if we take our half million a year and put 100 grand in investments, we can work for ten years and sit on the beach, only if we are willing to take a pay cut of $549,000 a year. Current interest rates at the time I am writing this book are 1.2% to 3% in savings and money market accounts. Best-case, that is only $30,000 a year in interest on our one million in ten years. Now what we did was buy real estate because it is free money. I will cover that more in chapter four.

A large part of selling 300% markup is attitude. Our cookware is the best in the world and has a lifetime warranty provided by the manufacturer. It is designed to save money in energy costs and in never having to buy another set again. So if you are going to sell at 300% markup you had better have value and benefits to your customer of 300% markup or more.

The old saying, "you get what you pay for", is very true. Buying cheap gets you poor quality products that will wear quickly and require replacement. So pick your product wisely before marking it up or you may never get it off the ground.

Remember to mark yourself up 300% also. What is your breath and life worth on a per moment commodity? After the murders of 9/11, you could ask many New Yorkers that question and they would tell you like the master card commercial PRICELESS. My time with my wife and children is priceless. I would never waste it on working for less than the million dollars that love commands it is worth.

This brings us to the whole concept of value and how to determine the worth of an item. Every moment of human life is a commodity for which there is no comparable material value. The worth of just one unique living human being is beyond measure in diamonds or pearls. How we markup our value is with self-esteem and the esteem we give to others in gratitude for sharing their lives with us.

I went to an art gallery once and saw a modern collection of paintings and other articles that were on display for sale. One of the paintings caught my eye as very similar to the artistic prowess of my three-year-old daughter. Curiosity got the best of me and I asked the price of the painting and was amazed to hear that it was offered for only three hundred and twenty five thousand dollars. So I asked the curator what commanded such a large price for this particular work of art. She began to explain to me how this artist had attended the finest schools in Europe and New York studying under some of the most renown in the art world. Furthermore, the market on this artist's works has gone up since the recent purchase of several of his works by famous persons. That is when the bell in my head went ding. It really didn't matter what was on the canvas. The color, shading, template, brush stroke, texture, shape, or what the work depicted had no bearing on the worth of the art. The value to me was zero, but the worth of the work was not measured in my value. This artists' work was worth three hundred grand because someone was willing to pay that much for it.

The same is true in real estate. An appraiser can value the market and determine the value of a house based on what the market shows similar houses in the same area are selling for. Here are some good ways to mark-up your worth in real world economic terms.

First you can move to a better neighborhood. Who you associate with and where you live has a direct correlation on work placement. Just ask any number of persons from any ethnic group in the poverty stricken area of any major US city. Income structures tend to remain similar in social groups and neighborhoods regardless of race.

Join groups, which expose you to higher income social groups. Join groups like historical societies, churches, and organizations, which may need volunteers such as art museums. Many higher class and economic level persons tend to be parts of these types of groups. I recently joined the Fraternal Order of Eagles, The American Legion, and the National Society of Sons of the American Revolution. I had the genealogy to prove that my forefathers fought and served in the Revolutionary War so this opened the door to new associations. This type of networking and development of new friendships can help in creating a high self-esteem and in common areas of interest, discussions on investments, plans, and goals. This is an excellent way to get introduced to an ideal mentor who can help you develop into a self-made millionaire.

Remember to have class when approaching these situations. Nothing turns off a person of wealth and fame more than to be goggled over. When I was a young man working at the Higbee Company in Cleveland Ohio, I was on the main floor one day talking to a girl that I was trying to get a date with. This girl had been somewhat aloof with me and I was not having much success with my invitations. As I was talking with her, a man rushed by us in the direction of the front doors. You see, this was Monday night football and Cleveland was the center of this evening's national broadcast. The young lady at the cosmetics counter whom I was wooing proceeded to say,
" OOH, That's Don Meredith, hey come here". At that point I said, " Who cares about Don Meredith, what about going out with me, Don isn't going to go out with you." Don turned around and said, " I like that man, he's got a great self image, go out with him" and continued on his way. The point of my story is that there is a reason

that famous and rich blue blood lines hate and shun the paparazzi, because they tend to goggle, get in the way, be inconsiderate, and interrupt life. Class is not just a way of walking, talking, and family history. Class is the worth you put in yourself and how you treat others around you. Class is a way of acting more than a way of breeding. To end my point the girl did go out to lunch with me. Later she was arrested for stealing from her employer. Perhaps the way she acted showed a flaw in her nature that happened to come out in her behavior at that one moment.

In the 1980's while at an Amway convention, I acquired a set of tapes about self-image, positive thinking, and pro-business ideas. These helped me throughout the years to maintain a can do attitude while in the military and in private life. What Don Meredith saw in me in that one instant of time, was that I knew he and I were no different. We put on our pants the same way in the morning, brush our teeth, and eat breakfast. It's what we do after that that makes us different. I knew since I was a young boy that greatness was in my path. My father had raised me to appreciate my family heritage and shared with me the ideas and stories of great men like Carnegie and Lincoln. He told me the stories of Marconi and how he was placed in a mental institution for believing he could send pictures through the air. We all watch TV because of this crazy man. As a young child my dreams became a byword in my family with which to criticize me, and my efforts when they failed. I did not give up. The only difference between Don Meredith and me that day was that he would be on TV at the football game that night. In my mind and his, I was just as much a star, just not shining so brightly yet.

Donald Trump shows this quality in his weekly show The Apprentice. He takes common American Dreamers and makes them stars. Reality shows are booming in this era because we have come to understand that greatness has no monopoly. We all can have the successful dreamer's attitude and the opportunity to be loved or loathed by America and the world in a half hour reality show. I think it was Zig Ziglar who said, " Whatever the mind or man can conceive and believe, it can achieve." If you think your great, you are, and you can achieve through hard work whatever your hopes and dreams inspire you to achieve.

Some other ways to gain greater self worth and appreciation for your abilities is to go to a dance class or finishing school. Many employers now are sending executives to classes on manners and chivalry in an upper class setting. Everything from art classes to music workshops can help you develop a keen sense of appreciation for society as a whole and build your self-image. One way to give and receive at the same time is to volunteer as an usher with the local theater. I saw Evita, Patti Labelle, and many other great shows that way while attending college. I also met a lot of people in the local arts and theater community.

Another outstanding way to appreciate your self and what you have in life is to volunteer at the Salvation Army. Go out with the food vans serving homeless and see what God has blessed you with, and remember, 'there but for the grace of God go I'.

Mark up the people you associate with 300% also. Encouragement and faith in another is worth a million in good will and achievement. When I adopted my son from Ukraine he had been belittled and ridiculed. He had little faith in his abilities and refused to go to school. When I asked him why, he said because I am a dummy.

Quickly I corrected him and explained that just because he was in a wheelchair did not mean he was a dummy. I explained to him how smart he really was and how well he already understood English in only six short months. I then proceeded to encourage and praise him on a regular basis, and mark him up with a positive attitude. In less than three months he was getting all A's and B's on his report card. When you get another to believe in what they can be you mark them up for success.
A few years ago a friend of mine asked me to help him film at the Cutco 50th Anniversary. The money was good and I agreed. Over the next few days I became amazed at the joyful nature of the employees and salesman working at this company. From the lowest sweeper to the secretary and Vice Presidents joy seemed to beam from this place. Then the time came to film the President Mr. Eric Lane. This man was the picture of positive attitude and joy. He was the best example ever that I have seen of 'Markup'. Salesman and employees recited story after story on how Mr. Lane knew their children's names, birthdays, and anniversaries. How he stopped by

22

their station at work and made sure they were OK after a short time off work for the flu. How he met them with a smile and a positive word of encouragement. He knows how to 'Markup' his employees. I heard the story of how he and a few others mortgaged their total livelihood in the belief of making Cutco and Vector work. From the recession of the 1970's, which almost closed down the plant, Mr. Lane has turned Cutco Knives into one of the greatest success stories of the late 20th century. His direct sales organization is one of the greatest to work with and no matter where you go in that company you will be effected by Mr. Lane's positive attitude. He shows his gratitude and joy in such a way that causes everyone around him to feel like a millionaire and his ability to ascribe worth in others marks-them-up in a way that makes them proud to have met him. The results are clear in that Cutco is a 200 Million plus company with a simple door-to-door sales force worldwide. Cutco's Forever Warranty and supreme quality make a set of their knives the envy of every gourmet chef. I own a set of Cutco cutlery even though my own catalog sells a competing brand. Perhaps that's because Mr. Lane made me feel what every one of his employees expressed they felt over those few days I worked there.

Marking up your self and those around you with a price tag of 3 million (3 times their life time income) will help you to put into perspective how much your employee's efforts are worth to you. If their potential is 3 million and they are only going to get one million that leaves you with the 2 million dollar profit. Treat them like they are worth millions in praise and appreciation and they will be eager to achieve the goals and demands that the job requires. You will be better off and happier when you learn that leadership is not just leading from the front. Lead by inspiration that changes the heart, by giving reasons for those who follow your dream to want to help you achieve your goals together. By showing compassion and concern about your allies and employees you build a firm foundation on which to create great wealth.

Thoughts and Ideas are worth millions

Who would have thought that a rock in a box with holes was worth millions? The pet rock idea proved that marketing was everything and a comical idea offered at the right time can make one rich. When I went to High School the word 'nerd' was a bad word and those labeled with it were the target of 'cool' kids ridicule. Now 'nerds' like Bill Gates are sought after for their great ideas and wealth. 'Geeks' even have a web site where you can hire one to help you with your computer problems. I am proud to call myself a four eyed pencil necked geek. I heard a General on TV after the first Gulf War say that it was the "Wally Cox" type proved to be the most successful in the new high tech Army among the officers corp. In my opinion it was also the Hulk Hogan type who fought on the front lines that commanded respect.

What was once an Idea, like lasers, now is commonplace in the hospital and the modern battlefield as needed tools to achieve sight and protection of our troops from hostile missiles. To think that when my father was a child that Flash Gordon comics had some of the first mention of ray guns, that idea became the modern laser. It is amazing how the pool of great ideas crossover into other fields of science and study to become real.

Perhaps you have an idea that can be used to build your future. One good idea is worth millions. A web site, a new gadget, a joke, painting, song, or anything marketed correctly can be a great return that puts you over the top. Many of us in America have heard the story of the college student who wrote a paper on starting an overnight shipping business that his professor said would not work. He quit college and started that business that is now FEDEX. That was a multi-million dollar idea.

In the 1980's in America you could hear the experts on the changes in the economy announce that we were developing into a service based economy. Slowly the NAFTA and global free trade treaties shifted the industrial workload toward Asia and away from the US and Europe. Today it is 2004 and the new buzz with the experts is 'outsourcing' jobs to India and other labor forces where costs are lowered in hourly wages. Profits are thereby raised for the investor in stocks of those companies that modify their work force to take advantage of this opportunity increase their bottom line. Liberals tend in America to treat this as an evil thing. But they are wrong. In this way we foster American Ideals and capitalism in other countries and expand and improve the world economy. Now when the people in India and China have more money to buy things, who do they desire to be like and buy from? The answer was given so well by a British businessman I saw on TV when he said, "I want those people to buy British products from my company". Those companies who see into the future of the world economy and market their products correctly to emerging markets will be in position to take advantage of the next phase of opportunities arising from the industrial economy and it's transition over the last 100 years. The new emerging economy for Americans is that of a reduced labor load, investor based economy. True freedom comes in reducing workloads and liberating individuals to be creative without the constraints of economic burdens.

When I was young, as with many young in America, my Mother told me to eat all the food on my plate because children were starving in China. Today I know that my Mother's love for me wanted to insure that I was well feed and healthy by eating all my vegetables. Still it somehow makes me feel benevolent that the products we sell in America are putting food on the table of billions worldwide. I am not ashamed of that. The Investor based economy moves closer toward the Ideal that both conservatives and liberals hold dear, to help their fellow man. By using our ability as leaders to create the next progression in mankind's move toward a unified effort of education, expansion into the universe, and stable economies in the global market, we become a blessing to others and transform our economy into greater freedoms. I should have entitled this chapter Ideas are worth Billions. The Ideas of global reach used with a solid plan like the one in this book, can be worth millions and billions when you consider the shift toward an investor based economy.

200 years ago America was like the world, an agricultural based economy. Just eating was enough work and we had no large combines to plant and gather food. In the 1800's the average person needed seven acres of land to provide food for one year for one person. Then the industrial economy took hold and the factories and new scientific developments brought the ease of workload concept. In the 1980's and 90's robotics began to take jobs away form factories and the service-based economy came into the world scope. Soon, the world will become an investor-based economy and acquisition of wealth will become the norm rather than the exclusive opportunity of a few. Once such ideas take hold, the creativity of mankind can be utilized to overcome problems and benefit all mankind in a mutual effort to industrialize space.

Agricultural development and Industrialization of space through new high tech methods can only be achieved by an elevation of the educational level and cooperation level of all the worlds' cultures. I call it the Babylon effect.

Virgin air is now offering rides into space. Soon you will see the need for the US SPACE FORCE to guard the planet from meteors and help rescue those stranded in space by emergency situations. Rapid space travel can get emergency services to earthquake and natural disaster victims in less time with greater life saving efforts increasing the rate of survival.

My wife is from Ukraine and when we go there to see our relatives it amazes me how all the young teens are dressing like Americans, playing American music, and learning English. When you talk to most of them they desire to come to America and become a millionaire. They have no doubt in mind that if they come to America, they will become a millionaire. What is the populous of those of us born and raised here missing? Having an American car in Ukraine means that you're very rich, or in the Russian Mafia. The young have integrated admiration of the USA with appreciation of where they came from and what the Ukrainian culture has given them in history and knowledge. Put them in America, and in less than ten years if they have any desire to be wealthy you will have a millionaire.

What does this have to do with this rule you may be thinking at this point, and why are you telling me this. To be successful you need a new idea about who you are and your ability to achieve greatness in wealth and reward for your creativity. Here are some ideas I am now giving to you. Did you know that a patent for magnetic propulsion uses particles of one charge to magnetically push a device with a ring of opposite polarity? You should search the US Library of congress web site and check out the patents that are pending. Perhaps you have a new thought that can change the design of an existing patent and can file a design patent that will benefit mankind in some new great way.

Don't Google over me was quite an expression for years before it became a web site. Why not choose some neat unique name or thought and buy that web address? I own several web address names and have several ideas to go along with them. The virtual untapped real estate market of commerce is the Internet and those who own and develop web concepts will be the multi-millionaires of the new millennium.

Napoleon Hill in his book Think and Grow Rich on page 65 explains how a large organization in the mind of one man became the US Steel Corporation. Similar people have constructed large wealth building organizations just from a thought.
There is one concept that I disagree with Napoleon Hill on that he lists in his book. He equates a Christian "Revival" to an action of sexual transmutation, as if such a thing existed. A Revival is the action of God's Holy Spirit acting on a person to create a deep psyche change of heart toward spiritual matters. Those who have not experienced it cannot properly understand it. The emotions and excitement of a spiritual experience has done more for mankind by affecting the history of the world than any other thing that has affected mankind. Channeling your energy out of love for others into actions that benefit others and your self is a creative action.

Hill is wrong in my opinion and the only place I know of where physical bodily functions such as his concept of sexual transmutation exists is in the fantasy mind of a science fiction thriller. On the other hand his concept of turning negative energy into positive energy and actions is what salvation is. Allowing God to forgive your errors and turning away from destructive behavior.

EBay was started from the Idea of a shipping bay on the Internet. Today Ebay stock was trading at around $100 a share for the idea electronic shipping bay.

In my small town there is a young girl who dropped out of college after a crushing relationship. She seemed to be depressed for a while and then a short time after she was her happy self again. She didn't seem to be working anywhere and she was spending a lot of time at home. Small towns like to talk and the rumors abounded over coffee tables and bar stools in the community. One day I ran into her at a store and we had a short talk about things and she began to share with me how she decided not to return to college because she didn't want to take a pay cut. I asked her what she was doing and she told me that she had started a business on Ebay and was earning about $250,000 a year buying and selling on the net. I congratulated her and said that is amazing. I asked her how she did it and she explained, "I just had an idea one day and it grew from there".

Thoughts and ideas make men go to Mars, businesses move products, and people write books. I like to add new books and home study courses to my collection on a regular basis just to see what new ideas are out there. The final frontier of man is said to be space, but I have heard it said that the space of which mankind shall best explore is between his ears.

A course I took some time back suggested that you keep a notebook beside your bed with a pen to write down your best ideas when you awake from dreaming. I find that some of my best ideas and thoughts come from that notebook.

I have a friend in the Country Music industry that writes music and has made a habit of recording himself in the shower. Some of his stuff from those sessions is comical and heart touching. Even so, I still believe it is a good idea to use every moment to utilize your brain's creative output.

In 1999 we (my wife and I) began our business and named it after my father, our son, and myself. R D J for Robert, Dan, and Jeremiyah. When working on a TV commercial to advertise our web site a friend asked me how we would convey RDJ to the people so it would be remembered. It took me a few days and a little thought about how to express our selves. Soon I thought of the great deals that we had in considerable savings over the cost of some of our items compared to the Malls. Then I saw a car commercial and the guy was jumping for joy because he got a really great deal on this car. Then it hit me like a brick in the face, Real Deal Jump. I went down to my recording studio and did a little jazz drumbeat and wrote a rap about the Real Deal Jump. In fall 2004 we first aired the RDJ Catalog.Com web site commercial and the rest is history. Stop by our web site and you'll get the Real Deal Jump too.

Madison Avenue marketing teams get paid millions for ideas like that one. Songwriters look for the same thing in a hit song. It is called the "HOOK", that part of the song or commercial ad that just makes you remember the rhyme, rhythm, and beat of the words set to music. The Hook or catch line that you just can't get out of your head because it is so annoying in some cases that you never want to hear it again. Many of those ideas stay in your mind forever. Like Coca-Colas' "It's the Real Thing". These ideas when combined with expert assistance in marketing can be the prescription to the illness of poverty.

Reading books and listening to audio books and tapes of business success methods is a great source of new ideas and motivation in the low spots. I used the Carlton Sheets Real Estate course 'No Down Payment' to invest in Real Estate. I used Ken Gaub's book 'Dreams, Plans, Goals' to set goals and write down plans for the success my wife and I have now achieved. Videos and CDs line my car's glove box and shelves along with books and cassette tapes from many varied business authors and motivational speakers. Whenever there is a seminar at a local hotel on new method of gaining wealth, I'm in the front row. Learning new ideas is free most times even when I don't buy the books or tapes. If Zig Ziglar is in town, you know I'll be there if they'll let me in. His techniques on sales always get me thinking and I think there is no greater expert on the art of professional sales than Zig.

29

Ideas are sometimes like diamonds. Like coal, you have to put an idea through lots of pressure, bury it under the tests of time, until the day the idea becomes real. Reading and putting creative input into the idea is like polishing the diamond until it shines so bright that you want it placed in a piece of jewelry to display to the world. That's marketing, it puts your ideas on display so the world can see the shine too.

An idea, even a good one, is worthless unless you do something with it. Alexander Graham Bell was a great example of how to act with class in a tough situation. After a suit over his telephone idea, he was bankrupt.
The fight had cost him nearly everything. He thought to give up the fight and give in with hopes that his great idea of communication worldwide would continue on to benefit all mankind. Then the truth came out that the one claiming his creation was a fraud. The suit was dropped and a deal with the Western Union Company was formed that made Bell a success. I always felt when reading this story that the reason God allowed this to happen to Bell is to see where his heart was. When he was willing to give the idea away in hope of mankind's greater benefit, he got his dream as a reward. Today we communicate on cell phones and write email all because of Bell's idea of communication. Bells dream has grown bigger than all his conception and no doubt become something beyond our dreams in the future.

There is one thing that I have learned about ideas, great minds think alike. Do some research before you launch your idea and make sure you have good advice from an attorney who is educated in copyright law and patent processes. Some of these resources are available on the Internet for trademarks and incorporating. The cost to get a US copyright from the library of congress is about $20 and the forms are PDF downloads from the web site. Protecting your ideas is not just smart, in today's world; it's a must to avoid needless legal battles.

Name searches and incorporating are good methods to protect your ideas. The services of a Trademark search or patent search attorney are less costly than a long court case.

No matter how different or miniscule your Idea may seem, jot it down, and review it with a trusted advisor. Together you will decide whether or not the idea is worth pursuing. Also realize that some of the greatest ideas were first ridiculed and shunned before becoming a successful venture. Before great inventions and ideas become the norm, failure will often precede greatness.

If one idea fails, try another and another until you find the business that God has prepared for you. Working toward your goal helps you be prepared for handling the success you will reap. If you want gold, you had better be willing to break the rock that encases it. God has a way to harness us until we are ready for the ideas he built our minds to create.

The test of our abilities and ideas, is the perseverance to complete the tasks we have at hand. Good ideas must be executed properly, and be accompanied by knowledgeable allies to make it a success. Having an accountant, a lawyer, a banker, and a host of business advisors to aid you with your ideas, is a must in the modern business world.

I have two attorneys, a payroll and expense accountant, a tax accountant, several loan brokers, bankers, insurance advisors, investment advisors, and media consultants. A host of wise advisors is a good thing, but in the end my wife and I make the final decision on what the next step will be. Trump says, "Be a general", but I think he forgot that the wife is the department of defense. Sales are the taxpayers that supply the real weapons of war in business.

Of course what do I know, I'm just a millionaire and Donald Trump is a billionaire. I bought his books because I keep expecting him to tell me some great secret on how to be a billionaire. His last book was great, but I missed the secret again. The *Art of the Deal* is clear enough, but most of us don't associate with the high society entourage that Mr. Trump does, and we don't have a TV show, yet. I see Trump has a new book coming out, "Think Like A Billionaire", I'll be the first to buy it.

I do enjoy watching his show The Apprentice. I find that many real life business situations are presented on that show, and the high drama makes for great entertainment. I don't think I would like to go on the show myself though, because I would have to give to many people the cobra-like "you're fired" when they stab each other in the back for 250K a year. The thing I love most about Trump and his show is that it proves week after week that with a little action and planning, you can make a lot of money in a short time. This past show, they had the corporate teams do a bridal shop. I learned a lot from that show, and was amazed that in just about a week the winning team made a profit of thousands of dollars. If they can do it you can too. It shows all of us that fact, and that is why I faithfully tivo that show every week.

As for the interaction between the players on that show, I hold more to the Zig Ziglar School of achievement, " you can get anything in life you want, if you help enough people get what they want." Trump has a great Idea in his show and in a progressive way, he shows the need to be tough in business while helping people get what they want.

Ideas reap rewards faster when you have the money to make them happen quickly. Trump's show demonstrates how anyone with the right attitude and a little start up cash can make good money with a solid team and expert leadership.

Since I started my ideas without cash, I have tried to stick to low cost startups to limit risk and increase rewards. Having ideas and thoughts are not enough if you don't do the work required to make them work. I talked with some of the marketing staff at the Carleton Sheets organization about why so many people order the No Down Payment course and don't do anything with it. One of the ladies said that she is amazed that people wouldn't use the course after buying it.

At first I thought it might be that some people are just lazy. Although that may be true, it seemed to be something more. When I talked with a local man who stopped by my store, he told me that he had the course also, but had not bought any real estate. I asked him why and he said, "I'm afraid to take the risk".

Many good ideas go undone because of fear. Now I don't take credit for this next idea, but I use it often. It is an acronym for fear that has helped me to overcome fear. **FEAR**= **F**alse **E**vidence **A**ppearing **R**eal.[1] Most fears are about things that have not happened when you're dealing with business. For example, let's say in sales you haven't sold anything yet or met the customer, because some are afraid to go on the call. It is the expectation of failure that is being reinforced with negative projection of bad results, or embarrassment of non-acceptance before rejection occurs.

It is best to face the fact that such fears are usually wasted mental energy, and best faced by doing. Action is the solution to bringing an idea to life and selling your product or service to the public. Practice will help you to dispel fear and give you confidence. An actor who knows his lines is prepared for the live performance.

In working with Ken Gaub doing his radio program entitled 'Faith in Action', it became clear to me that God had been teaching me to put my faith in action by doing. Faith with out works is dead. An idea without action is lack of faith. A positive attitude and can-do spirit is required to bring action and faith together with an idea, and create something of value for the world.

Edison is a great example of this point. He tried everything that didn't work on the light bulb and he didn't give up. From failure, fear was overcome, and light brought into the world. I like to say, the only way to truly fail is to never really try. For every problem there is an equal and opposite solution and for every adversity there is an opportunity for success. Some of the greatest Generals have been proven in battle when the whole tide of winning the war was at risk. In WWII, Patton moved his Armor forces faster and farther than anyone in history to win the Battle of the Bulge. Patton proved that the gravest situation was the greatest opportunity for success.

---

[1] The Acronym for Fear (**F**alse **E**vidence **A**ppearing **R**eal) comes from common usage in the general public which originated in the Alcoholics Anonymous recovery program and the author is therefore anonymous and has made no copyright claims to the acronym. It is in use as the title to several books and has over 87,000 uses in general therapy and psychological references.

There is no greater motivation in life to me than to hear someone say it cannot be done. I like the challenge, and see it as an opportunity that God has placed before me to prove them wrong. That is why I like to stick with positive people rather than the pessimistic crowd. You know the ones I am talking about; we all know one or two of them at work or where we worship. They always have a problem with someone or a discouraging word to say. They always create trouble and a gray cloud over any sunny day.

Avoid these negative people like a plague. Pray for them, be kind to them, but avoid them if you are going to let their attitude still your dreams. Your ideas will need every positive spark of creative electricity to come to life, and you will need to nurture it like a young child. Negative energy only brings negative results. Positive energy brings positive results. Jesus said it this way: " If you cast your bread upon the water, it will come back to you". He also said, " Cast not your pearls before swine". Notice I didn't say Steal your dreams. That's because people who will not change their mind and stop dwelling on the problem, but start dwelling on solutions, cause things to stand still. Amway millionaire Dexter Yager came up with the idea in 1978," Don't let anyone steal your dreams."

Dreams come true if you don't spend your effort on negative input. Ideas become dreams achieved with positive input and wise actions toward goal-oriented plans.
Write down your ideas and how you plan to achieve them. Make a list of what you will need to make it happen, and put a date on it when you plan to achieve it.
Then write down what you will do to celebrate, and reward yourself for your efforts.

Always have at least one more idea on the drawing board. I set goals that way so when I have completed an idea and achievement, I am not left without work to do.

Real Estate, Real Estate, Real Estate

We have all seen the late night or weekend infomercials on real estate and how you can become wealthy in the real estate business. I was skeptical like many of you when I saw these shows and wondered if it could be true. I watched Carleton Sheets for years before I ordered his course " No Down Payment". Today I kick myself for not getting it sooner. His course and software like The Real Estate Tool Kit, are solid, educational mentoring at its finest.

I remember my father once said, "They ain't making no more new real estate". The beauty of the real estate business is that we know that some of the richest men in America, and the world, got that way with real estate. The famous book, "Rich Dad, Poor Dad", by Robert Kiyosaki talks of passive income, or money that comes each month if you work or not. Rents are passive income. Robert Kiyosaki says that he learned this playing monopoly, four houses, one hotel, and it is true.

Now if you are in a similar situation as I was, with only $583 a month and some food stamps, then you will want to follow the method I used to gain a real estate empire. First, move to an area where you can get a house for $5000 to $10,000
If you are on the coast, you may need to move inland. Next, find a moderate economic area where you can afford to live and invest small to start out. If you follow Carleton's course however, you do not necessarily have to do this. I recommend this direction because it is the way I found the greatest success.

If you are disabled, you can get a subsidized payment for your own home from the USDA Farmers Home Administration or HUD. There are several programs on their web site to help homebuyers. Once you have your own home, restore it and add on to it as soon as you can. Then, get it appraised and refinance it for some equity to use for investing.

With the money you get from your home equity, buy a small home with an established occupant who is renting. You may find that you will not even need a loan to do this step if you buy right. Use the same method to fix up and appraise the rental home you purchased and duplicate the process. Using this method I acquired 14 properties in 2 years.

Another method is to find bank-repossessed properties that need refurbished, and buy them for very little money. After repairing the property, you can gain a profit by selling it or renting it out and refinancing it.

The next thing I did was to start investing in commercial property that has a good track record. Once you have been doing this for a while it becomes easy to make adjustments to your plans and methods to accommodate new types of property.
I recommend that you buy and use Carleton's course. He is not just a good mentor with a set of books and tapes or CDs to sell, he is also an investor who did it, then became a real estate agent and broker, and has documented students that have a net worth over 1 million.

I was enticed, finally, to get his course when I saw that he had taken a challenge to take people out in a city after a short instruction in his course and help them buy a house for no money down. The article showed that he was 100% successful with the three people chosen at random to participate in the challenge.

Here is where you will also need an attorney. You will need to insure that the property is free from any undue legal risks that only a real estate attorney can do for you. You will need a property insurance policy to protest you from loss due to fire and the like. Your attorney can also get you title insurance, which I recommend, to prevent you from paying for any errors in ownership or title.

Renters can be troublesome if you do not take precautions in some ways before intrusting your property to their care. There are many apartment owners' organizations that will do credit checks and background screenings for a small fee. This will help you to check on past rental history, and inform you if your potential renter has out-standing charges for property damages. Some states have special laws you will need to review to see what is required concerning rentals.

Landlord tenant rules vary in different states. Consult with your attorney before doing anything that will cause you to be sued.

HUD programs pay the rent for many of my renters each month. The check comes at the beginning of the month in the mail and I do not have to contact the renter to receive the rent. This is a great program to help the less fortunate and you at the same time.

Once you have mastered the small steps in real estate you can move on to developments and building projects. For starting rehabilitation projects, you can get some good books on home repair at Home Depot or 84 lumber that can instruct you in the basics of home improvement. They will also have lists of contractors to help with minor repairs that you cannot do your self, such as replacing water heaters or sewage problems. My disability prevents me from doing much of the work required to rehabilitate the properties I've purchased. I depend on my wife, son, and daughter to do much of the work, or contractors who have proven themselves to be honest in price and quality of work. I have been taken advantage of a few times by contractors who claimed to do things they didn't and the results are; they won't be contracted again. In turn, they lose the opportunity to profit from our current expansion of properties with our company.

My wife has become quite educated in applying wallpaper and laying carpet through this process, and has expressed to me that she enjoys making our rental units look special. My daughter and wife have become experts at shopping for home improvement supplies on sale, and converting the properties into nice, high rent yielding income. My daughter is a paint and stucco expert that can make any apartment or house a beautiful environment to live in. My son, Yuri, is an architectural ace, who can do electrical work, plumbing, and fine cabinet detail, and carpentry work. Many tenants and realtors have praised him for his finished projects. Appraisers have shown over and over the value of my family's efforts in real dollars. If you can do some work yourself, you can save money, use it for investing, and learn to repair something in a situation when a repairman would normally be called upon or is unavailable.

Another way to get below market real estate is to attend HUD or FMHA auctions. You may find, as I did, that in some cases the bidding is very competitive. Tax auctions are a good source too, but you must do your homework with these types of property to insure your not buying a headache with liens attached. Go to the courthouse, and review your potential purchases with your attorney prior to making any purchases.

Building projects can be completed with little effort if you have the patience to get through the red tape. Land in many rural areas is already zoned for residential construction, and in many cases, a bargain to buy. Acquiring blueprints for these homes are available at many home improvement stores. 84 Lumber has package plans that are built to meet code in your area, and building costs are a fraction of what the property will sell for in the right markets.

There is no better way, in my opinion, to build your net worth than real estate. Your net worth is the amount of money you would have, if you sold everything and paid off all your bills. Other net worth building ideas are collectable coins, collectable gems, stamps, historical memorabilia, art, and web domain names. Many shows such *as Cash In The Attic,* and *The Antique Road Show* have become popular ways to learn how to shop garage sales for treasures worth more than you have to pay.

Write down your possessions in categories such as real estate, collectable coins & bullion, and Art & Antiques. In the next column write a description. I like to write down what I paid in total cost for the item in one column. I put in the next column the market value or appraised value, then one for loans or liens against the item, and a final for the net equity of the item. A spreadsheet can be very helpful in setting this up. This way you can keep track of your assets and what your net worth is. Knowing your net worth is important for filling out paperwork for bank loans, to buy real estate, and measuring your success.

Owner financing is a great way to buy property. Many, for sale by owner properties, are willing to finance the property if you can negotiate a compromising deal. As for learning about ideas for deals, I suggest you buy Carleton Sheets' course. Here is one secret that is in his course I like to call Free Money Deals. I have put it into my own words and have read it in other books also.

BOND BASED LOAN FUNDING PROGRAMS

The essence of this idea is not a new one. Many financial institutions and governments have used this method to overcome reluctance of funding certain projects that present risk levels that may be unmanageable with conventional methods of lending. In spite of any reason restricting lending, whether it is for government or private funding, these plans can offer an alternative to seeking funding with higher than standard interest rates, and create growth to local economies, or adding to your personal net worth.

SLL (Self Liquidating Loans)

SLL's are loans that are tied to a bond ladder that have periodic payments, or balloon payments that liquidate interest and principal which yield funds free from debt and interest for projects in real estate and business. A popular form of SLL is the Real Estate loan where the principal and interest are paid in a single balloon payment, and funds are released at closing for project costs.

Example: A local government or investor secures US Treasury Zero Coupon Bonds in the face amount of 3 million dollars for $800,000.00 that will mature in 24 to 30 years. The bonds are then taken to an investor or financial institution that will lend 1.5 million dollars as a SLL that will pay the principal and interest in a one-time balloon payment of 3 million at the bond's maturity date. The 1.5 million is used to grant funds to local, low-income housing projects, or to purchase an income property that will help benefit the local economy.

Modifications to SLL's

There are two modifications to these programs that are often used to generate greater returns to governments and banks that are not willing to do loans such as those above.

The first modification is to have the bonds mature in a bond ladder that makes annual payments of principal and interest at graduated maturity. This type is restricted in that the amount of funds must be at a high enough level that the cost of bonds and fees are justified in the amount needed for the project. Funding requirements for Graduated SLL's should be no less than 1 to 3 million or the numbers at the current interest rate will not make it profitable for the banks.

The second modification is to have the borrower pay interest only or a partial interest payment. For small capital requirements, these types of loans become very profitable to local governments for community revitalization, or the rehabilitation of communities that have lost revenues from depressed economies.

Example: Local housing is in major disrepair that reflects on the view and attitude of a small city's attraction to business and manufacturing growth in the area. Many landlords and homeowners are negative about rehabilitation due to costs and fears of increased taxation. The city government then passes a bill that grants rehabilitating funding for local contractors to repair one to four housing units in the amount of $10,000 per unit. The bonds for this grant cost $3,000.00 and the interest cost is $3,000.00 if amortized over 10 years. The borrower pays back the costs of $6,000.00 plus a fee of $500.00 in equal payments over ten years. A local bank grants the funds of $13,000.00 in exchange for governmental guarantee, and the bonds at maturity are paid to the bank. The fee is a processing cost of $500.00, which is paid to the city.

This type of program can be used for property purchase funding for low-income housing, or to help local businesses grow through grants that can create jobs and fund city-works projects to create manufacturing or service industry start-ups. SSL programs can create a bed of funds that work hand-in-hand with business and the community to create a growth boom that will increase taxation to support services in the future and to offer temporary tax relief to inspire growth and job creation.

A local building in a major US city had come into disrepair, and was slowly becoming un-inhabitable. A non-profit organization was formed between the local owner and the city to grant bond funding using zero coupon bonds to fund construction and rehabilitation as well as tax relief for new businesses to form a cooperative development. The agreement made the city a part owner in the

40

project in exchange for taxes that would have been collected. This reduced costs for new retailers who would occupy the property when finished.

Local insurance companies funded the project startup costs with interest in the community and other large business funds for a percentage of the properties returns. The present owner was given a payment, for the property percentage that he was surrendering in ownership, and the city would resume a taxing position in 20 years.

Millions were used in the 1970's by developers to complete the project, and turn the old railroad station and offices into the Tower City Mall in downtown Cleveland, which is now occupied by such stores as Gucci and the Hard Rock Café.

While attending college, I first became aware of the Tower City Project working for Mr. Strawbridge at the Higbee Company in Cleveland. I used to walk through the old train station where water once dripped down and the lights failed to work. Viewing the major disrepair as a young man was depressing to see.

As a child, I remembered how my family and I boarded the trains in that station years before. Seeing it in the 1970's in such bad condition was depressing.

Recently I attended a manufacturer's meeting with the Scott & Fetzer Company in Cleveland, where we went to the Hard Rock Café in the Tower City Mall. It is so beautiful and amazing to see the contrast that has come to be a gem in the emerald necklace attractions to the Cleveland Downtown revitalization.

Many cities such as Buffalo could learn a great deal from Cleveland on how to develop waterfront assets, and revitalize downtown business.

The thing I like about the SSL is that for a small amount of money, with the right banker, you can make free money. Let me explain. You buy a US Treasury bond that will mature at a value of $30,000 in 25 years. You pay about $8,000 for the bond, and the interest is paid over the 25 years for the loan to the bank. In reality you rent the property for let's say, $700 a month. You pay interest at 6% and after expenses you put $300 in your pocket each month. In three years the renter pays you back for your costs *and* the interest at the bank. You see? Free Money.

Here are some things to keep in mind when using SSLs to invest in real estate:

➢ Have the bonds first. Banks do not like the scenario I have seen in some books on the subject where the bank loans funds to purchase bonds at closing.

➢ Foster the relationship with the bank first by loaning money and paying it back in a short time of 6 months to a year.

➢ Work with the same bankers with each of your deals. Knowing you can go along way when you need an ally in your corner.

➢ Give your investing time to prove your abilities. A track record of 2 to 3 years of paying mortgages on time goes a long way before you approach them to do an SSL.

➢ Graduate into larger projects in smaller increases in size an effort needed to manage the tasks. Learning by way of hard knocks can help you know which contractor is unacceptable and which is proficient by working with them. You will also learn how to hire and train along the way with smaller projects. This experience is vital to help you build a successful operation as you grow.

➢ Find partners with experience in these types of deals to help or take part in the project. Having an advisor who has completed this type of transaction is a great tool to help get it done.

Now, I did not come up with this idea, I got it from Carleton Sheets who passed it on to me in the form of a home study course. The reason I write of it here is to stress the importance of getting good information from the form of continuing education, to help you get wealthy. Many community colleges have short continuing education classes in accounting, real estate appraisal, and a host of other courses that can help you get the knowledge you need to learn how to deal with experts you will work with.

You can often find acquaintances that will loan you small amounts of money to help you get started in exchange for a percentage of the profits if you do the legwork to network, and sell your ideas for investing to others. Loan brokers are a great source for finding private investors who will fund real estate projects when the bank won't. The Small Business Administration also has help sources that can get you in touch with Angel investors who will help with small business projects.
They will even give you an advisor who has retired from business to help you. To find out more go to SBA.GOV

I borrowed $10,000 from a private investor to get one of my first houses and paid him back with interest in less than 3 months. When you get a track record for returning funds quickly from your profits, it becomes easier to get others involved in your projects in the future. Good news travels as fast as bad news in these cases, and I make it a habit of asking them to give me a personal reference in the form of a letter signed by my happy investor to take to the next investor. Having a portfolio of references is a smart tool on the road to building a millionaire empire. Trump writes of this in his book, pay back your investors,
word of mouth advertising works just as well with negative as positive. Your reputation is most important on the road to success. Don't burn the bridges in front of you.

In one deal, I did some advertising services for a fee and turned the fee around for a down payment on buying his rental properties. If you search hard enough you will find these types of deals also. Once people in the area know you are investing in real estate they will begin to call you.

I work with several real estate agencies in my area looking at properties and making offers. Now many of these brokers call me and tell me when they have a good deal they think I would be interested in. I look for deals on the Internet too.

You can build your net worth, rehabilitation, rent or resale real estate. In less than 24 months if done correctly, you should be earning at least $4,000 to $6,000 gross in monthly rent. I base that figure on my own experience and effort. I did it in an area of Pennsylvania that has a below national norms in income and growth. By finding the right properties and using HUD Section 8 subsidized renters. Buying one to four unit properties is easier because above four units you need commercial financing. I feel it is best to start small and grow large when first starting out. I don't believe in the get rich quick methods that over extend your abilities rapidly. It is get rich slow that builds wisdom to deal with the tough calls along the way.

One of the greatest ways to get free money under the tax code system is to harvest your equity by borrowing against it. The interest is tax deductible and loaned money is not income in most cases. You should check with your tax advisor because tax laws change all the time. By borrowing against our house, my wife and I got money to help in our rehabs, and it made us more money in return than it cost.

Making money from equity is a great way to start an investment plan also. I use an online broker and trade my stocks myself. E*Trade has automatic order entry so you can place orders to sell or stop a loss that will take effect even when your not watching your stocks.

Stocks are a great way to participate in the businesses in America. My wife has a self directed IRA with E*Trade and that is a great way to prepare for retirement. Your tax advisor or a broker can help you plan for tax liability and advice on investment programs. There are risks involved with any investment program, and that is why I like to have control over my investments.

Adding investments to your efforts over time can help your net worth and can be fun if you learn how to day trade. Buying low cost stocks that limit the risk in dollar amount and selling them when they move up a penny or two.

I bought a genetic stock company that traded at eleven cents a share and held it for three hours. When it went up to twenty-two cents I sold and made $110.00
That might not seem like a lot but if you learn how to do it, you can do that all day long with the right stocks and earn far more than working at a factory.

I bought that stock at $119.99 and after commissions, I made $80.00
Had I worked that day in the best job in my area I would have made $77.00 after taxes for an hourly wage. Sometimes you have to work smarter, not harder.

I don't put a great deal of my cash into the stock market because I don't want it subject to extreme risks. Dividend producing stocks are a good way to go when you have built your cash flow into a large enough amount to start growing it.

Overall real estate is the safest pace in my mind to keep the large cash. Its dividends in equity and rents are not altered by some opinion or market trend.
My rent won't go down when the Federal Reserve Chairman speaks on TV like some stocks have been known to do. The Securities and Exchange Commission has done a lot to help make the market a safer place to put your money, but in my experience, real estate yields a greater return in a shorter time period. Besides, I am no expert at stocks and have no training in that field. Ask a broker, they are the experts in that area.

Savings are the start of all transactions

Who said it first I do not know but I remember hearing my father, who was an accountant and salesman, say it often, "never underestimate the power of compound interest". If your goal is to acquire wealth in great amounts then you will need a savings account. Most Americans do not even have $500 in a savings account. Many financial consultants say you should save at least 3 months income or the cost of three months bills. When I first heard that I said, "Yeh, right".

Now I have accounts with several banks and keep my cash in interest bearing checking accounts, mutual funds, money market accounts, and a self directed IRA for my wife. Another account I have is an investment account with an online brokerage. I suggest that you have at least 5% of your total assets in cash and investment accounts within 5 years of starting your life as an investor.

If you are worth a million then you should have at least fifty thousand or more in accounts. This is a good start to insure that you will not be late in any bills, and can handle any emergency needs such as when a furnace goes in one of your houses.

If you are on welfare like I was, you will need to start slow with a passbook savings account. My wife and I saved and collected cans to start our savings. We took them to the recycling center and put at least half of the funds into a save and do not touch fund. Eventually we had enough to start an online brokerage account with $500.

I then bought some US Treasury Zero Coupon bonds and held them until the profits were enough to pay for the commissions and give us a return of $200 after expenses. Then we had seven hundred, which may not seen like a lot to you but to me it was a start. We used five hundred as hand money down to buy our first piece of real estate. When you have some savings in the bank it makes the day go by easier. You know that you have a safety net in case. You should consult with an investment advisor on any type of investment you

46

choose and they can spell out for you the risks and rewards. With any type of investing there are risks.

When I was a child in Cleveland, Ohio, it was not uncommon to see young, African American children shining shoes for money on the streets of Downtown. It is a great statement of the improvement of our culture to say that is a rare thing to see today. When talking with an old friend about this change in our culture he shared with me a story of a child we knew in our neighborhood that was known to go downtown and shine shoes for some spending money as a child.

It seems that he did not spend all that money he made in manual labor after all. He had been putting it into a savings account and when he went to college he had over fifty thousand in his bank account with interest. During college he took that money and bought inner city houses, which his father helped him rent, and he paid for his tuition with rents and grew his assets. When I asked my friend what happened to him he explained that he moved to France where he became an investment advisor for an international company making a six-figure income. He sold his houses later at a considerable profit and now he was living large in Europe.

From the age of ten to twenty this child with a savings account planned for a future that many never believe is possible. He did it by saving a small amount and letting the interest grow.

It is said that Rockefeller kept a small book in which he wrote every expense into a ledger, recording where every penny went and how much savings he had. His ability to know where his money went no doubt helped him to keep track of the vast empire he created in later years. Savings is the foundation of all transactions and keeping track of where your money goes is a good way of seeing how to control your spending.

I keep account of all my spending including small purchases such as lunch and even if I buy a drink on the way. I save every receipt and keep them in files for the accountants to review monthly. It is important to know where every penny is, and what your buying habits are to plan changes in behavior. Reviewing your spending can help you to find new resources where you can cut costs and build your efforts toward economically healthy actions. By saving a few cents here and there you can build it into a vast fortune by maintaining control of spending habits. Place those funds in savings accounts and watch the money grow.

Part of savings is to have a budget to work form. Pay yourself an honest living amount on a weekly basis, and keep the rest in savings until needed to pay expenses. As bills become due, transfer the money to your checking account and pay the bill. By doing this, I have been able to pay our house payment three months in advance. I also add a little to the principal each payment to save on the interest over the long run. A big part of savings is to save on the amount you are paying for things like your own home. By paying down the principal, the interest costs are lowered, and the time left to pay off the house is decreased.

With real estate investing you can reach a point by acquiring enough properties where you can begin paying off a mortgage every so many months. When you get to property number 25 to 50, you start having a cash flow of about ten to twenty thousand or more a month. In two months you can pay off a twenty to thirty thousand balance on one of your mortgages. Eventually your savings helps to remove all your debts and your savings start to grow by large amounts on a monthly basis. When you reach 100 or more units, you can begin buying homes for cash and save on interest costs all together. By duplicating your efforts with each month of your investment plan, you can soon retire and enjoy working for yourself.

Here is a chart that may help you see the beauty of this method of savings and investing.

PROPERTY	COST	MORTG.	PAYMENT	PROFIT	TOTAL
Property #1	10,000	8,000*	200	200	200
Property #10	120,000	82,000	800	2000	2000
Property #20	250,000	170,000	1200	4200	4200
Property #40	320,000	280,000	2600	8440	8440*

By property forty in our example above we can now pay off property number one. By property number 100 we should be able to start paying off and buying properties for cash. Using proper saving methods should help you to earn monthly income above six figures in ten to twenty years with a constant effort. At 100 properties, you should be at or near twenty thousand in profit a month, and well on you're way to earning over 500K a year gross.

Once you have succeeded to the level you desire you can put your property in the hands of a management company, pay your self a reasonable income, and go fishing with your family. Today, I work when I want to, and spend a lot of time with my children and wife. Having a good savings gives me the ability to do that.
The only thing stopping you from doing it is to begin. I love the ancient Chinese proverb that says 'the journey of a thousand miles begins with the first step'.
The bank account with hundreds of thousands of dollars begins with the first deposit.

One of the greatest savings plans for long term investing is the US Treasury Zero Coupon Bond. To reap a reward of $1,000 in 24 to 30 years, one bond will cost about $200 to$300 in the market at the time I am writing this book. So to get $1,000,000 in about 30 years you will need approximately $250,000

If you are just starting out of high school or college and you purchase these bonds on a monthly investment plan, you could reach that simple conservative goal in about twenty to thirty years. A 25 year old would have one million by age 55.
I am not expert on stocks and bonds. I am not a stockbroker but I do invest with E*Trade online. Here is what E*Trade writes in their information on bonds in their knowledge center:

"Yield vs. Risk, Inflation risk, credit risk and prepayment risk are all figured into the pricing of bonds. The more risk, the higher the yield. It's also true that investors demand higher yields for longer maturities. The reason for that is obvious – given enough time, a once-healthy corporation can go bankrupt and suddenly lose the ability to pay its obligations. Inflation could run rampant, seriously eroding the purchasing power of that $1,000 you're supposed to get back in 30 years. These things are unlikely or you'd never invest in the first place. But the longer you tie your money up in a bond, the more at-risk it is statistically. The credit quality of companies and governments is closely monitored by the two major debt-rating agencies: Standard & Poor's and Moody's Investors Service. They assign credit ratings based on the entity's perceived ability to pay its debts over time. Those ratings – expressed as letters (for example: Aaa, Aa, A, etc.) – help determine the interest rate that a company or government has to pay when it issues bonds. The market determines the price – and thus the yield – after that."

That is one of the reasons I invest and save with E*Trade online. If I have a question that I am not an expert on, I can get the answer in less than 5 minutes by going to their Knowledge Center. Wherever you choose to save or invest, Bonds can be a great way to get rich slow.

Never seek money above Love or others

Many have been heard misquoting the Bible saying that money is the root of
all evil. The exact quote is: "The Love of money is the root of all evil".

To love money above people is what causes evil actions that are selfish and ill conceived. We can see the news stories every day that herald the cases of murder and drugs that are examples of this. If you are doing something that is not benefiting others and your family just for the money, then you need to do something else.

Take responsibility for your own actions, and do not blame others or find excuses, because if it is immoral then it is going to harm someone. The porn industry earns billions. It is harmful and dangerous to society. Famous porn star Marylyn Chambers exposed the evil of underage porn in the industry and now has a non-profit organization called children of the night that helps get teenage girls off the streets and on the right track.

Recently in the news I heard a story of porn stars that contacted aids from a filming in California. You may get rich that way, but at what cost? Do you want your daughter to appear in a porn movie? I don't!

Factories who pollute the environment and poison the community in which they operate may make money for a while, but in the end they will have to answer for their crimes and pay for their evil.

As a believer in Yahshua (Jesus), I do not do anything that will harm another in the pursuit of riches. Sometimes that means tough love so you don't contribute to another's self-destructive behavior. One of the left coasts liberal media attitudes that has got me steamed is the idea they present in film and the press that if you are a person of faith, you are crazy.
This nation was founded by men of faith who believed in God and had respect for faith in a creator who blessed us with freedom. I saw

Phil Donahue on Fox News before the election and was repulsed by his bashing of President Bush's faith in God. Phil scoffed at it saying." He hears voices". I do too Phil, the voices of over half of the millions of Americans who love God and Country and voted for President Bush. We don't like your comments on us and we are not as dumb as you would like to portray us.

We men and women of faith are not psycho murders who beat our children to death like is seen in some movies. We men of faith are not dumb rednecks who drink too much and cheat on their wives. Oh I am sorry, that would be left liberals who cheat on their wife in the office of the Presidency.

President Bush is a great man who loves his wife, Laura, and you can see it in their eyes when they look at each other. Perhaps that's why they get attacked so much. I think that the liberal media and democrats are jealous of a traditionally married couple in love. When you sell out your morals for power and money it shows, that is why Kerry lost the election. It was our slap in your face that says we don't care what you think in the liberal communist media, we work for our money and don't share it for your immoral causes because we tithe at church. We give to the Salvation Army and the Red Cross and help those in need rather than give them a crutch of excuses to continue unproductive behavior because the government hand out will pay their way.

I like that our President had tears in his eyes on national TV after the murders of 911. A man who has a heart and thinks of the mourning of others and is not afraid to cry and show his emotions is what this nation needs. I can see in my mind he and his wife crying together alone and praying for this nation. That is love in action.

I don't like that one of the biggest contributors to the Kerry Campaign was a billionaire who wants to legalize drugs in America. I would like to see those liberals in the detox centers holding an addict while he pukes his guts up or is being resuscitated by doctors. I have been there when men and women's drug addicted bodies have given up the fight and died.

If the Democratic Party ever hopes to have any power again in this country they had better abandon the idea of making drugs legal. Why, because they have placed money and power above the well being of people.

In a recent airing of the Rebel Billionaire, a young women walked off the airplane to give up her chance at the presidency of Virgin Atlantic Corporation because she knew she would have been unwilling to do what the task to advance on required. I would hire her in a heartbeat. She understands what sacrifice is, which I believe is a greater asset of love, worth more than doing some dangerous feet is worth. Some people just don't get it. She not only 'Gets it' she is it.

The Bible says, "No greater love has any man than this, that a man give up his own life to save his friend." The stone cold hearts of some people is frightening.

Love of others over self is what makes this country great and it is what will make you great if you are true to it's calling.

When you truly love others more than yourself you become willing to do what is required to build wealth and become a benevolent member of a family, society, and the community at large.

" We do not fight against flesh and blood, but principalities and powers, spiritual wickedness in high places." Spiritual wickedness is easy to see if you watch out for it. It runs in the face of danger. It lies to get its own way. It steals, murders, gossips, and it has dark consequences in its inevitable end. The efforts of those who seek to legitimize what God has made illegal will not prosper in my home and the left cannot make me agree with what is wrong just because they put judges in office who seek to put an end to God's law.

I think that the Chinese people will soon be a free people in government and society because of their ability to resist in silence. During their cultural revolution they hid their musical instruments when music was outlawed. After the climate in government changed back to a more intelligent view of music and its value in society, the hidden instruments reappeared.

I often think that the liberal left, in-your-face-angry, democrats own the true intolerance of different lifestyles in America. They cannot stand those who believe in God, and the law that says you will have to answer for your sins.
It is because of their sins that they refuse to face their errors and seek forgiveness and repentance. Love would willingly forgive and give a better blessing in life if they would only repent.

Unnatural behavior and evil is a product of lust rather than love as the left wing claims. True tolerance of some sin is illegal in many cases. In the state of Pennsylvania it is illegal to not report child abuse if you have knowledge of it. That is a good law and should be upheld.

Putting material gain or power above others is not a solid wealth-building tool. To really gain wealth, you have to put others into your formula before your self. No product can ever be marketed unless you put your self in the buyer's shoes to learn how to best meet their needs with your product or service. By working as a team you can gain wealth that gives you the ability to contribute to those who are less fortunate in constructive programs and charities. America has been blessed throughout the years because of the efforts we have made in taking our wealth in knowledge and money and helped other societies in the world become more self sufficient. We have fed children in famine and war torn countries. We have programs such as the peace corps that helps people gain insight into different world cultures and lend service to other needy nations.

Love is not selfish. Love knows how to become a benefit to others and not squander the wealth on selfish ends. The true rewards that come from sharing is the happiness that you see in the eyes of those who are helped by your benevolence.

In my state they have a program called the Special Kids Network. It is supposed to help children like my son who has Duchene's Muscular Dystrophy get help for their special needs. What it really does is provide some information on who to call to get help with an 800 number and pay high salaries to politicians friends for managing what you could get cheaper by dialing 411 or surfing the internet. Not one dime of the money for this program helps any child to my knowledge and my son, when he needed it, got nothing from this program but a run around.

In contrast, there is a benevolent group in our area of the southern tier of New York and Northwestern Pennsylvania that has a program called the Big 30. This charity football game gave my son checks for special needs equipment on several occasions when he needed it.

When liberals come up with grandiose social welfare programs to help others, hold on to your wallet and investigate whose friend in the campaign is getting a job. Private faith based agencies do more to help than any government agency could ever do.

The MDA is a private nonprofit organization and they have helped my son buy three wheel chairs.

When researching where to send your contributions after you become a millionaire keep in mind that the real agencies give and publish their finances on giving direct to those in need.

Having been on welfare, I know that if the government got out of the way and cut the middle management costs and red tape, millions would be saved in tax dollars and increased benefits to those who really need it.
I do not object to paying taxes for social welfare programs that help people gain a foothold on a new start when they need help out of poverty. I do object to the programs that waste tax dollars on unneeded efforts.

As you gain wealth do not forget that there are others who have needs, that your help will be the only lifeline saving them from hunger and sickness. Love demands that we give as we gain on the road to financial wealth.

In this book you may find that I receptively write the same thing in a redundant way. That is because I learned that the mother of memory is repetition. In college I would often write down key points to study for a test on index cards and read them over and over until I had memorized them. Read this book over and over to learn what this book has for you in ideas that will benefit your efforts to reach your goals.

If you love someone, you want him or her to succeed. Success is a product of pride and self-worth coupled with a sense of self-esteem when you are teaching others to achieve greatness in life. Seeing others use what you have given them to achieve a goal, award, or recognition helps to reinforce your own self-actualization in life.

Love is not selfish, the Bible says so, that is why one should give help to others if they hope to achieve the true riches in life. Once you reach your goals, mentor someone else into their dreams and goals.

Poverty is a mental condition

Some of the people I have encountered in the social welfare system are brainwashed into believing that the system is the only way they will eat. Some, due to mental illness or physical handicap, can only depend on the system for their life supply. The subject I am addressing in this chapter is not about those who are unable to work. There are some that cannot and then there are some that could if they wanted to. Those who are able to do some sort of work, and are unwilling to leave the safety net of welfare are the ones who I am addressing.

When we opened our store at Bradford we hired some people for direct sales and some became successful. We hired many who were on welfare, and after a paycheck or two all of them were gone. They didn't show up for work or came up with some excuse why they could not work. One young man in particular impressed me and I talked with him when he picked up his last check and asked why he quit. What he told me was typical of the problem with the system and how it is designed to keep the poor on the welfare roles. He said that if he earned too much, he would loose his SSI and food stamps. Now this was a young man who was only about 22 years of age. Yet he feared success even in the face of earning over $1000 a week. That is $50,000 a year and he would rather have SSI at $600 a month and some food stamps along with a Medicaid card.

Many of the people I meet on welfare have a common problem, which I call the mental condition of poverty. They want the system and the government to be their mommy and hold their hand. One guy had his four kids on ADHD drugs and was on SSI because he was violent and could not get hired. He would get a job and when the boss would tell him to do something he would go off and hit him.
When you look into his past you find out that the reason this guy was so angry is because he was raised in the system. He had learned to get what he wanted by acting that way so he found no reason to deal with his temper and get help.

The system was enabling him to keep him in the system so the social workers have a job creating the problems that they say only they can solve. The problem is that the social workers have been in the system so long that the only way the regulations allow them to deal with the problems is to be part of the problem.

The attitude of which I am speaking is only changed when the person has a change of heart and is taught how to live. What the system needs is a deep overhaul and not just workfare classes and job training.

There are some people who like to complain and have jobs. They sell themselves short by believing that someone else is smarter or better than they are. Their negative self-image places them in a small paying position and they rarely rise above the poverty level. Their mental conditioning keeps them in a comfortable place where they will stay poor.

This welfare mentality is a mental condition for which there is a cure if one makes the effort to overcome their fear and take action. If you are on welfare and have bought this book and have gotten this far then perhaps you are ready to make a change. The first step is forgetting all your excuses that you call reasons for not succeeding. The reason people are poor in the USA is because they choose to be. Don't lie to yourself that it is because mommy or daddy did something or your teacher or the police or anybody. It is because of you that you are where you are.

Today is the first day of you living in the now. Yesterday is gone and tomorrow is not here yet. So what are you going to do now to make your future poverty free?

When I was in the ARMY we didn't consider going home until our mission was complete. Getting the job done was a matter of honor and commitment for America's freedom. We didn't whine and cry about it. We just did it. Success was not an option it was the way we did things. There was no fail. We didn't complain that the enemy was verbally abusing us either. Cause we knew that the reason we did not fail was called lead poisoning, from a bullet out of the enemy's gun.

One of my favorite Star Wars lines is when Luke Skywalker says he doesn't believe it, and Yoda replies, "And that is why you fail". To get off the welfare mental condition you've got to believe that it is bad for you, bad for the country, and that you can do better for your nation and your wallet.

In the training classes we give at our office we teach how to sale products, how to meet people, how to knock on doors, and how to overcome negative attitudes with positive attitudes. Most of those in the system want you to believe that you need them so that they can keep their job. So to rehab welfare you need successful business people to volunteer some time and go down to the welfare office and teach people how to change their attitude.

During World War Two, which my father fought in, there was rationing of food and goods so that we could win against the evil murdering fascists Axis. People had victory gardens so they could have fresh vegetables and the can goods could go to help our troops overseas. They sacrificed to help us win. I wander if today that same spirit would bring us together to win against a foe such as our parents fought?

They didn't know fail. They didn't whine. They just did it. Women worked in factories, which was unheard of before then. They got blisters on their hand and one fine lady I know personally made mortar rounds during World War II. Her husband was in the Navy fighting in the pacific and she was packing gunpowder into shells. Some times things went wrong in that plant and women died making bullets. They didn't get a purple heart or a metal for what they did. They knew that if they didn't do it that they would be enslaved for the rest of their lives under Nazi tyrants.

Their mental condition was one that had only the goal in mind. Fail was not an option. They had no choice. To be on welfare means that you have failed if you can work. Can you answer a phone? Stuff an envelope? Type?

If your mental condition is negative change your mind. Ken Gaub in his books writes it takes a millionth of a volt of electricity to change your mind. To be positive you must have goals and dreams.

59

You must write a plan down on paper and when they say it can't be done, don't believe them. I teach my children to never use the word can't. It is a dirty word that means you won't try.

There is a saying that I love to hear because it is very true and worth repeating.
'If I give a man fish, he will eat fish today. If I teach him how to fish, he will eat fish every day.' When I was on welfare I fished and caught food for my family.
One day a man came by and talked with me and said, if you need some food you can come up to my house and clean some chickens I'll kill for you and your kids to eat. So my wife and I went up to his place and we had chicken for a month.

That man saw in me that I was doing everything I could to get food for my family and that I was not letting my disability stop me from doing anything that God required me to do. Feeding my family was first and he wanted to bless me with some chickens.

God has always watched out for me like that. When I needed something he has sent angels like that into my life to help. Once I had just started a new job and I had no food or milk and no money to pay for any. My wife yelled at me in the morning and commanded that I talk with my boss and get a small advance so I could make it to my first paycheck. Walking out the door I told her that God will provide for us and that she should not worry. I had not locked my car doors in such a rush to work in the morning and in all the business of the first day on the job it slipped my mind to ask for anything. I left to go home and realized that I had forgotten to ask my boss for an advance when I came upon my car and it was full of food. Now I'm not just saying a few bags of food, I had a station wagon and it had twenty or more bags of food in it. I ran back into work and asked my boss who put all that food in my car? She said that she did not know and asked me if I needed any gas or milk money to help me until I got my first paycheck.

Two years after that happened I ran into a preacher that asked me to help out with the food bank at his church. It dawned on me that he might have been the guy who God told to put that food in my car, so I asked him. He said that he was just driving by that day and heard

Gods voice in his head say intuitively, "put some food in that car." I proceeded to tell the preacher that it was my car and the story I have just told you and we thanked God for teaching us both a lesson. God watches over us and sends his agents to help when we are in need.

I guess what I am saying here is there is a difference between using the system and needing the system. To many who are using the system are able to do something to help themselves and are unwilling to work to get out of the system.
Maybe what I do in sales and real estate is not for you. There are SBA loans to start a business that is more suited to your likes and other programs that can help you get out of the system.

Willingness is the answer to most problems. If you change your desire toward being willing to learn something new and educate your attitude into a positive outlook on life it is amazing what you can do.

When I began my quest to gain wealth, I wrote down my goals and how I was going to achieve them. I made a one year, three year, and five year plan and put pictures of what I was going to do with the money I had earned from my efforts on the refrigerator.

This book is one of the goals on my list of things to do this year. I feel it is important to share my ideas with others to help change attitudes and contribute to the community with positive thinking.

Zig Ziglar says that we enjoy the benefits of success. In my training classes on sales, I like to touch on this concept by explaining that we do not pay the price for success as some say. Rather we pay the price for failure. When you cannot pay your bills, feed your children, buy them what they want and need, that is paying the price for failure. When we learn to earn a fare profit for a quality product or service we learn to enjoy the benefits of success.

In the next chapter we will look at how millionaires train their mind to achieve goals. Identifying poverty as a choice and a metal condition is like tilling the soil of your mind to plant new idea seeds that will grow into money trees.

Millionaires visualize their dreams

"A man without vision will parish", The Holy Bible. If we have no vision we will die. In a package of sales flyers I received from a sales training company there was a flyer about John the ordinary man. John's obituary reads on this comical flyer: Born 1900 Died 1921 Buried 1999. He like many in the negative worldview live out there lives as walking dead men. John never took a risk or believed in anything. He scoffed at starting a business, put down his children's dreams to be great star actors or musicians, and successfully crushed every hope that came near him.

My children have a habit of asking my wife and I about anything and everything on their mind. The ground rules are clear, no boundaries just ask. So when my daughter asked about modeling, I got some information and she researched the field and found that she was interested, but not enough to move into it at this time. I have from her youth told her she can do anything she set her hearts desire to do or be as a profession, as we have with all our children.

Encouragement is hard to come by in today's world of harsh critics on subjects from music to acting. Writers, Chefs, Sports, and many professions have their critics that evaluate and are suppose to be experts on the subject. I have a habit of going to the movies that have bad reviews just because I like to buck the critics and see for myself.

No matter what anyone says about your dream, if God wants you to have that dream, and you will do everything required to achieve that dream, it will come true. To build my attitude I have made a habit of doing what I like to call dream building. I write down what it is that I want to achieve and then how I will do it.
With monetary goals I also include a picture of what I will do with the money when I get to the goal. Each year I do this and have goals on my refrigerator, bathroom wall, office door, computer screen saver, and in several places. Each time I see them, I read them aloud. I keep a copy of my goals in my brief case and look at them often.

Why? Because I read somewhere that millionaires visualize their dreams and goals and write them down.

I call it Dream Building. To project into your mind positive results as if you have them. For several years before I bought any real estate I went to my fried Chuck at Rocking Horse Realty and looked at properties. I wanted to see what I would be buying and do the legwork and learn in the process. I asked him questions and he helped me to understand.

For years before I got a sports car and a big SUV I went to the car dealers and look at and drove the cars out of my price range. I wanted to feel what it was going to be like to drive a car that cost more than $50,000 and get use to the idea that it was going to happen. I call it Dream Building.

Exercises such as the ones above are simple ways to train your visualization process in the brain to accept that it is normal for you to be rich. Look at the million dollar houses. Test-drive your dream car. Put pictures of them everywhere. Write on the pictures 'my car on ' and put a date there.

Close your eyes and say a prayer. See your self in a boat near the shore of a tropical island. Visualize you are there. Put a picture of where you want to go on your desktop. Look at it ten times a day. I call it Dream Building.

If you do not build a dream and visualize where you are going and write a plan on how you will get there, the chances are you will never do it. My Mother had a dream of going to Ireland. I must have heard her day 50,000 times "Oh, I'll never be able to afford that". Guess what, she was never able to afford it. Why? Because she kept saying it over and over and she eventually believed it.

I loved my Mother and would have loved to take her to Ireland. She passed away in 1998 and was in poor health in the last seven years of her life. She taught me many great things and I honor her memory in many ways. But the truth is that she talked herself into failure lots of times. It finally dawned on me a while after she died that if she could talk her self into failure then maybe I could talk myself into success.

Guess what? It works! I went to Disney World last summer. Took the kids too. Spent lots of money too. I had my Mickey Mouse pictures on the dream boards all over the house. I call it Dream Building.

I went to the jewelers about 100 times and asked to put on the Rolex. I was almost thankful when the salesman I got didn't know me when I bought my Rolex. Wearing it every time I went to the mall was so cool. And Now I own one all day long. I call it Dream Building. If you don't see your self in it, you won't make yourself get it. I call it Dream Building. My wife calls it dream shopping. She has spent a lot of money in the malls over the last two years. She was just filling all her dream orders and fixing up the house the way she wanted it. She got some really hot clothes too. So did all my kids.

When I go to sleep at night I have a little mind game I play. I call it Dream Building. I put myself in my mind in a big beach house in somewhere like Coral Gabbles. Then I look at the ocean, turn to look across the marble floor where the sun is reflecting toward the door way with a drink in my hand. Then J Lo and Madonna walk in with drinks in their hands and my wife says…honey wake up!
I call it Dream Building.

My point here is that you have to see your self as someone who would hang out with the Bling Bling and do the great things in life. You want to be a star, act, do it. See yourself doing it. Become what you want in your mind and you will make it a self-fulfilling prophecy. I call it Dream Building.

Put your goals in front of you always and you will teach your mind to see yourself the winner that you are. Millionaires and Billionaires have learned to do this over and over in America. I call it Dream Building and it is why immigrants over seas have said in years past that the streets of America are paved with gold.
Why do you think it is that so many live here all their lives, and never acquire wealth? Yet we see immigrant families come to

America, work together in a restaurant or other business, and become very wealthy. It is because they jointly see the dream together. They have been visualizing that dream for years working hard to get to the USA and make it happen. The desire to turn their thoughts into reality and achieve wealth, and their own business, has etched itself into their heart and brain.

Seeing their dream become real was inevitable. It was built thought by thought over years of waiting for a visa to get here. It was painted in pictures in their mind that, once here, they would work together to be millionaires. Dreams like these have no choice they just come true.

$100 bills cost the mint 6.5 cents

The United States Treasury prints this thing on paper we call money. It is worth only the cost of the paper, the ink, and its material components. One Hundred dollar bills, according to the director of printing and engraving, cost only six and a half cents to make and are in reality worth only six and a half cents.

The reason money is really not worth anything is because a few years back we went from a gold based economy to a debt based economy. That is when some economists began to understand that the world had been playing a game called money. Money is not real. Money is fake; it is a game, like monopoly.

What is true is that we all have collectively agreed to play this game called money. Even communist China is playing now. And they are doing pretty good at the game lately. It is important that we are all going to play the game by the rules.
Money has rules and we have to play by them.

In the game of money, money is not the object, things such as houses and cars, businesses and stocks, are not the object of the game either. The object of the game money is control of things like businesses, houses, factories, hotels, and the means to produce and sale bling bling that comes along with those things.

If money is not worth anything then getting it should cost you nothing. The truth is that it costs very little to get money and it costs everything. You must put yourself into the task at hand like it cost you everything and once you get the rewards of your efforts it will seen like it cost very little.

Unless you were born rich, you will most likely never be able to earn a billion dollars in a lifetime form your own personal labor. So if you want to be a billionaire, then you have to find a way in your lifetime to control assets worth a billion dollars without earning it through your own labors. As a millionaire I control assets today as I am writing this line worth about five million dollars. I owe a debt on those assets that reduces the asset value to about three million. Yet in cash today I only control about fifty thousand dollars.

If I was to go to work today for a company I could sell my self as an hourly or salaried slave to a company for the price we agree on. Perhaps because of my position with my company as president of the corporation, we may reach a figure of one million a year or more. Yet as you read this you may be of equal weight as I am. You may be of equal height and educational background as I am. You may be on your way to work for minimum wage or thirty thousand a year reading my book.

What makes that so? You are no different than I am. We are of the same species and form of frame. What the difference is that makes me worth more is that I have played the game and presented my piece of the playing board as worth more.
The rule about money that so few get and win the game with, is if your presentation is fine-tuned to sing like a symphony orchestra, people will believe the packaging they see. The other half of that rule is you must believe the packaging to sell yourself at that price.

$100 bills are accepted to be worth one hundred dollars because we have all agreed in the game to accept the packaging that reads $100.

So repackage your product to catch the eye and you will sell your self for a higher price than you have trained you mind to believe in the past. Add a zero on to your package value. The difference between 100 and 1,000 is just a zero, 10,000 is only a few zeros more. 1,000,000 are just a few more zeros or places of nothing, which is what zero is equal to. We are just changing the accepted packaging. When you bought this book what did you buy? Packaging of a certain order of words that you believed will help you gain riches, isn't that right?

What if I told you that my book you are now reading will add nothing to you at all. You will have to add it to yourself. Just a few zeros and some fancy packaging? You can do anything you want in life if you're willing to. The rules that I use for this game called money are right here in this book. The titles of the chapters are those rules that the world has used and agreed upon to play the game.

We have appraisers who say given the cost of a square foot of construction, and a piece of paper called my license as an appraiser, and that houses in the five mile area sold for this or that price, therefore it is worth $500,578.98 or what ever number they think they won't get sued over. That is the money game. It is only worth that because we agreed to pretend that money is worth more than 6.5 cents.

Earlier in this book I talked about a 121 Karat emerald that my wife owns and that it is appraised at a given value. It is just a rock. We paid wholesale for it. It is worth a whole lot more than we paid for it. Because we played the money game and got an appraiser to value it and certify that it is worth more, we could auction it off somewhere for that price or maybe more.

Art works the same way and so do most things like antiques, collectable classic cars, coins, and your own self worth. So add some zeros to your self worth and repackage your efforts and be a millionaire. Everyone else is imagining that you are what you have presented to them you are. Shakespeare said it best. " All the world is a stage, and we are but the players". So act like your worth more than that and don't let anyone sell you for less than what at least you will earn in a lifetime. You're worth more than the money in your pocket but you're value is exactly what your self-image of what you are worth is.

Why did all the Enron and WorldCom executives get arrested? Because, they cheated at the money game and got caught overvaluing assets and themselves and in this country that is called, in the money game, illegal. Governments have written rules to the money game called laws. You must lean to follow those rules in order to win. If you do not you will have to surrender it all and go to jail.

When we began selling cookware we set our goal in multiples of 10 by zeros. We paid ourselves $100 a set sold so if we wanted to add a zero we needed to sell 10 to get $1000 in commissions. Thus to get

$10,000 we needed to sell 100 sets. To get $100,000 we needed to sell 1000 sets. To do that we needed to hire 5 sales persons to sell 20 sets a month for ten months. That is what I call the money games rule of ten. Increase your efforts by learning to add zeros into your production and you will reap larger profits.

Real estate is appraised by a similar method or the rule of ten. Generally you can know if you're paying the right price for a property if you take the profit before mortgage payment on annual bases and multiply it by ten.

The illusion of value in money has been addressed in modern banking in efforts to move toward a cashless smart card or biometric method of accounting for the barter of goods and services. I personally, due to spiritual convections, would not participate in any biologically permanent marking system of accounting. Keep my computer chips in the computer or smart card please. The Bible strictly forbids any mark in or on the right hand, arm, or forehead in connection with the transaction or identification of persons for the purpose of selling and buying. I do not object to a cashless barter system as long as it is not bio-implanted as a permanent fixture to or in the human body.

Money is acquired in multiples of zeros, which makes it imagined to be worth great assets. The reality is that the power to control assets and your believing that your have the ability to manage those assets is what is worth more than all the worlds possessions. When you use the rules to your advantage and get the bankers, brokers, sellers, buyers and bosses to agree with your self worth, then you will win and be the millionaire that you already are. Or of course you can continue in the game and like Trump and Gates and become a billionaire too.

The winner in the game of money learns to place himself or herself in a strategic location in the money cycle where they can best use their assets to reap a percentage of the profit from the constant transactions around them.
Money is going to change hands everywhere in the world you go no matter what you do. Learning to place your efforts and packaging in a location where societies recognize you as an obvious receiver of a

percentage of the profits is a plan driven marketing strategy. Products or services you offer must appear to be equal or grater in value than the value of the money customers spend to own your product or services.

Affordability and knowing your target market is another great factor to consider in the money game. You would not try to sell a Rolex for five thousand dollars to a blue-collar worker who earns minimum wage. You must market to the audience that can afford to purchase your product.

One way to make your product affordable is through financing or reoccurring charges to credit cards until the item is paid off. Many American companies do this to help consumers purchase high quality products valued above their means.

The presentation or packaging that attracts customers to your product must meet their approval. Advertising and marketing programs that address target market in demographics and outlets that get your message out will prove to be successful in the money game.

There are three ways to market your product or service to the world. All routes are only variations of these three ways. The three ways are, direct marketing, mass marketing, and passive marketing.

Direct marketing you go out and advertise in the customer's home or knock on the door and sell your product. Mass marketing you get the customer to purchase through a toll free number and sell indirect to the customer. Passive marketing you open your store and wait for someone to walk in to buy what you have.

The most successful winners in the money game use all three ways to get income.

It can be completed in stages to allow for budgeting and cost controls. When you look at the most successful retailer, Walmart, you can see the perfect plan in action. Walmart has store front operations in your community, a web site, and TV and print advertising. They sell on affordability by offering items of medium quality or better at low prices. To win at the money game you must have something that people want that is presented in a convenient location in their life where they will feel comfortable in purchasing from you.

The Rich Dad Poor Dad program also deals with some of these concepts in business in the area of passive income. Renting real estate is a passive marketing program that means it is low cost to advertise. It is also a passive income in that very little is required to insure the income continues when you are unable to work. Everyone needs a place to live and pricing your rents in the market at an average according to the price your market can bear ultimately insures success.

The old saying in business is true. There are three things you should remember when starting a business, location, location, and location. You can add the next things from our discussion would be that the packaging and presentation must catch the eye and bring income into your venture.

Some food for thought is that the total printing cost for one million dollars in one hundred dollar bills is only $650.00. The Federal Reserve Bank has packaged that $650 with the value of $1,000,000.00 and we buy it every day of the week.

Now if you understand that money is a game, an intangible concept, with which we use to barter for things in exchange for efforts and ideas, then it is easy to start to practice agreeing with concepts that will bring you wealth. In other words money is not real. The concept of money gets us control of the real stuff.

Give and it shall be given unto you

Pat Robertson wrote of certain laws, which are in the Bible that cause a person to become wealthy. Many such as Norman Vincent Peal have written on the power of positive thinking. There are certain laws establish by God that have proven to work for the good of society and in causing blessings in my life.

The law of charity is that you give, and it will be given back to you. I know that this works in my life because you get something of value when you give to help others and they do not know where it came from. I don't announce it or talk about it. I just keep it to myself and let God keep the score. The joy in self worth is better than the money or gift I give anyway. Giving helps to build your self worth and ultimately increases your positive attitude and self-image. When you feel better your body releases positive pheromones that attract people to you. That makes you feel even better and you become more effective as a result of the positive effect.

Find a charity that deserves your efforts and volunteer time, tithe money, or give of those items you no longer need. My wife and I give 10% as a rule to ministries that help feed the poor or provide medical life saving medication to those who cannot afford it. We give above that amount in offerings for special gifts when we feel that God wants us to.

You may not be God oriented as I am. Still God will bless you if you follow his laws and most Americans feel it is our obligation to benefit society in some form of giving. The 10% rule will be helpful for you or you may want to participate in some program such a Christian Children's Fund. There are lists of charities that have independent auditors who verify how much is given to the stated purpose of the charity. You can check with local clergy or an Internet search to find valid charities. I make it a rule to never give to telemarketing charities. Many of these are hired for Police agencies or organizations that get very little of the actual money given. Locally we have a volunteer fire and ambulance service. I try to make it a habit to give to those organizations directly to insure that needed services are there for obvious reasons.

You will be surprised how things positive come back to you when you do something positive for your fellow mankind.

There is a misunderstood law in the Bible that most of Christianity teaches the opposite of. God has set in stone for a blessing, a law called the forth commandment. It is the Sabbath commandment. If you go to the original commandment in the Hebrew Old Testament the commandment translates roughly like this:

On the seventh day rest, read my word, Pray and do Gods Pleasure. Do not buy
or sell on the seventh day. Do not work on the seventh day. Don't make
anyone else work for you on the seventh day. This is a sign that
you are following me and that you are my people forever. If you rest on the
seventh day, I God will bless you so much that you will have more than you
need. You will have houses and land, cattle and children and grandchildren.
You will own great possessions. This is an everlasting eternal covenant.

There are some who have changed the meaning of this commandment to read a subscript that equates to 'only if you are Jewish'. That is not what appears in Exodus chapter 31 or any reference to this commandment in the Bible.

In the 1990's I had a disagreement with a popular minister on this matter. This minister thought that I was restricting worship to only the seventh day. Worship of God is permissible every day; God commands rest on the seventh day.

Some argue that we enter bondage by resting according to the law as New Testament believers. Last time I check in the dictionary work was a type of slavery for which you get paid. Therefore, if I am set

74

free for one day which God Commanded freedom from work, then that is not bondage. The human body needs time to replenish its ware from work and think about something other than the worries associated with life's labors and finances. If you are a Christian, the seventh day rest will give you replenishment for Sunday worship and help to discipline your spending habits. One day a week out of the malls and traffic will not hurt you. It will most likely reduce the stress in your life. Doctors say that stress reduction is good for the health of your heart. So even if you are not keeping a Sabbath for religious reasons you are doing your body good to rest.

At the end of the Old Testament, the Minor Prophets write that when Messiah the great high priest comes, the entire world will rest on the seventh day. So I look on this as good practice for following Gods directions and preparing for Messiah's return. A strange thing happened when I started keeping the Sabbath rest, I got blessed.

I was in Walden Book store looking through the section of books on success and wealth building and ran across a book by a Jewish author and glanced through the pages. I wanted to see what he was saying about why God blesses many Jewish people with great wealth. Near the middle of his book there it was. God promises blessings when you give to others and rest on the Sabbath. The word Sabbath means rest. My own experience is that you feel better by resting one day a week and you work better and more productively by allowing your body and mind to have a time to replenish itself for the next six days.

Some doctors have said that the human body runs in cycles. Biological clocks and patterns that we are subject to. Once I discovered that my wife was running in a monthly cycle that was why she acted the way she did at certain times, it became easy to map those cycles and know how to plan for changes.

Every woman goes through three cycles a month. Like a bird in the wilderness those cycles are the primping, nesting, and empty nest cycles. During the primping cycle she will make herself look good. She will be loving and flirtatious.
Then she will move into the nesting cycle. Clean the house and work and build the nest. Then she cleanses with the empty nest cycle.

Every man should study this 30-day cycle of emotions if he hopes to have a successful marriage.

Men have the same type of cycle in energy and emotions they just rarely show it.
By resting on every seventh day, you lessen the highs and lows that are effecting your biological cycles and allowing the body to repair it self for the next cycle.

So give back to God what he gives you each new day when you wake up, some time.

Dress the part, lead with your heart

Some years ago a book came out called ' Dress For Success'. Popular TV shows are doing makeovers of all kinds on prime time that draws the ratings. The bottom line is that if you look like a bum; don't be surprised if your treated like one.

A suit and tie may not be required for every occasion but style and class is important. When meeting with your banker you will want to wear a suit and tie.
When you are looking at property you may want a pair of casual jeans in case you need to get dirty checking out the mechanicals.

When you first start out you want to watch for sales. Go to the deep mark down rack and get the good stuff cheap. If you don't know how to find it, find a woman with children that you know shops smart and ask for some help.

Salvation Army and similar types of stores often have great clothing that can be made into a presentable outfit or suit that will help you until you can earn some profits that will get you some clothes. If you are planning on selling, just a shirt and tie will do. If you are going door to door, try not to make it a white shirt or you will be mistaken for Mormons or Jehovah Witnesses.

And old suit coat got me in a door one day when the guy said he felt sorry for me because of what I was wearing. That gentleman bought my product and gave me $100 besides. I was thankful in that this is when we were first starting out and that money helped. Garage sales are great sources of clothing for very little. In the rural area where I live, 25 to 50 cents is not unheard of for some good clothing in a yard sale.

Know your target audience for the presentation of you clothing is also important.

You would not show up to a funeral in a wedding dress. Dress the part. You are packaging yourself for success and you must play the part in the generally accepted norms of what successful people have in their wardrobe.

You must also meet the standards of the social situation in appearance. Leaving the tongue ring at home for a day or taking it out for a few hours won't hurt as much as getting the piercing did. Being successful may require that you conform at least for short periods of time.

Your importance and status will only be portrayed in what you look like, what you say, and how you say it. If you have a conviction in what you are doing you will lead with your heart. Understand that the person you are dealing with has to play be the same money rules you do. Being rude or combative in difficult situations is not going to help you achieve your goal. Presenting your self in abstract images is not going to get you there either.

Be nice and show a friendly nature. My Mother use to say you catch more bees with honey than vinegar. You want your buzz to be sweet not sour when you're spoken of behind your back. Take time to smell the roses on the way and the wait will be more enjoyable.

When it is time to get the top of the line products to wear, a fashion consultant is a good thing to have. You can get suits that look like they cost thousands on sale for hundreds at the right stores. Don't be afraid to shop around and see what style looks best on you.

Attracting other to you should be your goal here. Look attractive and act attractive.

What you are seeking here is to market yourself and gain allies through networking to market your products and services. You must first have a product or service that you believe in. If you do not believe in what you are offering then it will come across in your presentation. So find a product or service that you whole-heartedly believe in.
Part of the marketing game is to learn the art of persuasion and salesmanship.

I teach all my new salespersons to use the psychology of sales techniques in communication and presentation of our products and services.

There are several writers who go more in depth on this subject and I highly recommend them. Zig Ziglar and Tom Hopkins are among the best that I have found to help you learn how to say the right things in a presentation to get the sale. There are a few phrases I use and teach that are easy to learn and can be used in many situations to persuade your customer or potential ally to be sold on your product or you.

They are: Isn't it, wasn't it, Couldn't it, Shouldn't it, isn't that right, and don't you think that's true. The natural response to these phrases is yes and that is the goal in any sales situation, to get you customer to say yes. Another phrase is wouldn't you agree. If I can show you how to talk people into buying your products or service, you would practice putting it to work for you, isn't that right? If it would make you rich, wouldn't you agree that it is worth trying?

Sure you would because the natural response to that question is yes. Learning how to work these persuasive techniques into your communication helps to create a closing situation that will result in selling your goal, product, or service to the target market.

Be excited about what you are doing. Did you ever try smiling to every one you pass by on the street? It rubs off and they smile back at you. When you are pleasant and excited about what you are selling the customer gets excited also.

Dismal monotone presentations get dismal results. Excited presentations get exciting results. Watch some late night infomercials and you will pick up a lot of sales persuasion phrases. Things like 'your' new cookware. This usage of the word 'your' is meant to build ownership and get you to think about the product as yours. Notice how the British accent guys are so excited about that mop, orange cleaner, or vacuum? These are techniques that are meant to catch your attention and get you excited about using that product.

An old ad had the phrase 'see the USA in your new Chevrolet'. Combined with hooks, which we talked about in an earlier chapter, these phrases can be powerful things.

Getting a person to like you and want to be around you is a natural part of our being. Women especially, have a natural ability to make people want to know them. They take hours sometimes in preparing their physical appearance.
Often they think quickly on their feet to come up with the right phrase or words to get just what they want. Many of us guys go out of our way to accommodate their desires.

Appearance, communication, and presentation help to form an image in the mind of your associates and customers that can lead you to successful encounters with those who will help you achieve your goals. People like a winner in America and you can present yourself as a winner by showing them a winner's attitude and package when you lead with your heart and dress the part.

Humor is a great set of clothing to put on in any sales presentation. Where it with a matching smile and clean apparel and you may find as I have, that people will buy your product because they first bought you.

True success is not measured in money

You may not agree with some of the political and spiritual beliefs that I have expressed in this book. But I want you the reader to know that I sincerely believe in those views and that the best way to deal with many of the problems in America today is to hold on to some of the traditional values those beliefs express.

Wealth building, sales, and the knowledge of how to acquire wealth are ideas which need to be taught in our public schools so that many of those in the society who are unproductive can find a joy in life by having there needs met and feeling self worth by helping others.

The best form of the communist ideal is the capitalist who is benevolent with his wealth. Unfortunately, the communist practice has always been corrupted by greed and abuse of the system and resulted in the mutual sharing of poverty leaving the masses of people in despair without motivation which gain creates.

Ownership of the means of production is not evil, as some would have you think in the political arena today in America. By owning wealth-producing ventures one can employ people who would otherwise not have a living. Some people are just not able to lift themselves out of despair of the drudgery of negative attitudes and see the light and joy that life can be. Most times that is because they don't' want to.

It is beyond me that Foundations have given great wealth generated from some of the world's most well known capitalists to NPR that is one of the most left propaganda producing stations in the world. NPR preaches communist and liberal left ideals like we all go along with that failed system.

My wife lived in Ukraine under the communist ideal. She lived from hand to mouth in that system with no hope of getting a better life or greater education because the system was established to share nothing. People who don't own things don't work very hard for nothing. That is the problem in France today.

Once you hire someone in France the system is so ingrained with communist ideals that you cannot fire them if they are not productive.

President Johnson's Great Society has failed and there is no hope for such a welfare state that invests its livelihood in non-productivity. That would be like paying some one in a factory who made the least the highest wage. Eventually the company would go bankrupt.

Still we see in the liberal media the hate of corporations preached like some great ideal that they assume we all go along with. We are the corporations. We own the stock that pays wages to workers who buy products and services and all of us pay taxes that provide the safety net to those who are honestly unable to work.

I enjoy looking at the web sites that track where George has been. You know, the dollar tracking web site that is written on some of the bucks we get in change.

Our capitalist system is a lot like that dollar bill. It gets into many hands and makes many people wealthy to some degree along the way. When you think about it, that dollar gets spent a lot of times before it makes its way back to the mint.

The economic circle of life is creating growth in this nation and for those of us who have lived long enough to see it, growth worldwide. Our capitalist ideal has for years provided over 60% of the worlds food supply. Why didn't communism do that? If the sharing of poverty had been successful, then it would have kept the old Soviet Union alive.

Why are so many leaving Cuba? Just today on the news there was a story about an entertainment group in Las Vegas that came to perform and were able to convince the communist dictatorship to let them come here. They were not here very long when the whole show applied for asylum. Maybe we should ship some of the NPR staff to Cuba to live in exchange.

The truth is that the ideal that the Democratic Party holds to is in root and practices a communist idea of the mutual sharing of poverty. I first heard it explained that way by Ronald Reagan. I not only agree with that opinion I observed that as a fact in the 1980's on the iron curtain. I saw it in practice in the Soviet block of nations.

Teaching entrepreneur ideals and wealth building methods that help build economies with the strength of ownership is the best insurance we have against poverty and the best help to eradicate it. Success is more than money, its what you can do with it.

I believe that given the heart of the American people, that when wealthy, they will help their fellow man. I don't think I need the government to budget my money into programs that would not produce results. From Roosevelt to Carter we had the ideal of big government controlling our pocket book. It did not work.
The tax rate was 70% when Reagan entered office.

You may be wondering what all this has to do with that thought that true wealth is not measured in money. Well, I'll tell you. When President Reagan past away, you didn't hear people saying he was a rich man. I saw a piece on how he started in a lower middle class home in Illinois with not a penny to his name. I saw a piece on how he had a defining moment in history when he said," Tear down this wall".
I even saw a piece on TV about how he lifted our nations spirit and brought the patriotic heart back into our people.

In 1982 I was at the Iron Curtain and gathered with some other soldiers to pray beneath one of the cement towers, which lined the razor sharp fence on the East German side as far as the eye could see. We prayed that day that God would open the door to the east and bring down the Iron Curtain so we could give Bibles to those under communist rule. In 1993 I went to Ukraine with the Bible league and did just that.
As a result I found the love of my life, my beautiful wife Olga. I cried when President Ronald Reagan died. It wasn't for what he had; it was for what he left behind.

My best friend was Jerry. He and I socialized and when I needed some help with immigration, his wife being from Ukraine also, he helped me. He was the best man at my wedding. He died of skin cancer and left his wife over a million in insurance and investments. At his funeral no one mentioned that he made sixty thousand dollars a year. No one said that he had a big 401K or IRA and left his wife rich. The preacher did say that he helped a lot of people and that he believed in the messiah.

What we leave behind in example and gift of love not measured in monetary value are worth more than diamonds or gold. President Reagan opened the door with Gods help to answer my prayer and give me a wife. Jerry prayed with me to accept the Saviour and helped me to keep my wife and family in this country.

Both of these great men were my mentors that left behind a lot more than all their worldly possessions. They both left me with inspiration to aspire to be something more. True success is not measured in money, but in what you leave behind.

You can't take it with you

A blue-collar worker was in the hospital and on his deathbed. He didn't regret his life because he had three wonderful sons that he had helped through college and were well off. He called his three sons into his hospital room and said to them,
" My sons, all my life I have been a hard worker at the factory and yet for all my efforts, the most money I have had in my pocket at one time was only a thousand dollars. As my final wish, I would like you, my sons, to place in my pocket a thousand dollars each after my funeral so I can rest in piece as a rich man." The three sons agreed to their dieing fathers wishes.

On the day of the funeral after the service, the first son who was a doctor, went up to his fathers coffin and placed one thousand crisp one hundred dollar bills in his fathers suit coat pocket and said, "There you go Dad, rest in peace."

The next son was a dentist and he went up to his fathers coffin and placed one thousand crisp one hundred dollar bills in his fathers suit coat pocket and said, "There you go Dad, rest in peace."

The final son was a lawyer. He went up to his fathers coffin and wrote a check for three thousand dollar and said, "There you are Dad, now don't cash that check until I put the other two thousand in my bank account tomorrow, or it will bounce."

I first heard this joke told a little differently at a Kirby sales convention. I do not know who the original author is but it illustrates an important point here. You cannot take it with you. So you had better make plans now while you are alive to protect your assets.

You will need three things for this part of your planning: A lawyer and insurance agent, and a banker you trust. I know that is a large order in some areas of this country, but I have already told my lawyer joke so we won't go there.
I am not an expert in this area but I will share with you what I have done in my state and why I did it.

I had a living trust drawn up so that my assets are protected for my children in case I am unable to function in the final years of my life. My wife and I incorporated our company so that we could give our children shares of our income producing assets in the shell of a corporation so that the taxes can be paid now instead of when we die. Inheritance taxes are too high and will crush our assets destroying the stability of the company if we had not done this.

Next we bought long tern care insurance and life insurance. If you are forced as my mother was to go on Medicare to pay for your nursing home stay, and you have any assets you planed on leaving to your children, forget it. The social welfare system will liquidate your inheritance and spend it on your care costs.

In our state a living trust can be controlled by your banker who will help increase assets and fight to protect them from taxes after you are unable to handle your own affairs. Find out from a lawyer what is the best course of action in the state where you live and if they tax you 33% like in my state you will want to place assets in other locations so that they can be better protected.

The Bible says that the parents lay in the storehouse for the children. Don't be greedy and leave your grandchildren without a remembrance of who you were and your love for them.

Roth IRA's are a great way to place money in educational savings accounts to insure that your grandchildren are educated. The tax benefits are great also.

You should have a tax advisor to help instruct you in what you should do each step of the way. I use H&R Block, which in our area is also Fox Financial Service. They offer in many locations the same or expanded services including home mortgage and refinancing. They have a great insurance policy you can purchase when they do your taxes also. I recommend it and buy it because it insures that if you are audited that they will pay any penalties and go with you to the audit.

I have been audited once in my life and do not wish to do it again. Most of these IRS workers are naturally in a bad mood and when you got money and come in for an audit it just reminds them that they hate their job. So naturally they take it out on you by pulling tricks and trying to trip you up on admitting to something they can get a penalty on. That is what they are taught to do in the back rooms with their supervisors. Most times, because the code is so big, if they want to they can make you pay more. So I won't do my taxes anymore and suggest you do the same.

Many banks can manage trusts and real estate for you as a trustee. Don't do what one gentleman in Pittsburgh did and put it in the hands of a lawyer without getting a second opinion. After he died it was in the front page of the paper how the lawyer had written in to the document his complete control of his assets. The lawyer gave all his great wealth to the Catholic Church. His wife and children had nothing and the law could do nothing about it.

Insure that the safeguards are in place with any will and trust so that the beneficiaries are getting what you intended them to have. Checking the bonding and liability policies of whom you are doing business with is a wise thing to do also. If they refuse to give you the information then I would not do business with them.

Plan for your charities also and put them into your will and or trust. Having the money go in reasonable amount to help to establish foundations is wise.

On TV the other day they had an interview with one of the original investors in AOL when it was first starting out. He is said to be worth about 160 million today. His original investment was only about ten or twenty thousand dollars.
He has established a foundation to help others and has given money to help the DC school system.

Bill Gates has a foundation and even Mr. Trump has worked hard to provide benefits for charities and for veterans groups. His contributions from his wealth and efforts to help society are renown and commendable.

Establishing these foundations and trusts before you leave this world to sleep is something to many leave until tomorrow and it is left undone when needed.

I did not want the court to decide how my assets would be divided. That leaves to many opportunities for my children to argue when they should be celebrating my life work and having a party to send me off.

I believe what the Bible says that we should rejoice at the passing when your work for God and mankind is finished. That is something to celebrate in my opinion.

I have been at a lot of funerals in my days where the major drama going on is a fight over the assets of a loved one. If you follow the directions in this book you will avoid a lot of hurt feelings among family members and have sufficient wealth to insure that you leave everyone well compensated when you are gone.

Dream Big, Think Big, Live Large

In the 1970's there was an economic rescission in the United States that was in large part caused by a negative attitude. This had culminated into an effect in business and real estate that was reflected in the landscape of the New York City World Trade Center resulting in a large number of vacancies. During the decades of construction dreamers such as David Rockefeller and others had looked far forward in hope and faith toward a prosperous future for the Twin Towers. Planners had not foreseen that needed special something that would market a mass affection that many in New York had for certain buildings. The Empire State Building had the ambience of several movies and the Hollywood glitz of meeting that special love on the observation deck. This was not yet for the World Trade Center and in many ways it was looked on as an oversized elephant of an era gone by. Little known to the Port Authority, a dreamer had his eye on these twin giants with an idea that would change the view of New Yorker's and the world about how the WTC was viewed in their hearts and minds.

Some years before a young man in France had taken a different view of the gigantic twin sky scrappers in the place so nice they named it twice, New York, New York. This man had no care for the fact that he lived in another country. He had no thought that the buildings would someday be struggling to get tenants and become profitable. He like no other man on the face of the earth at that time was on a mission that only a dream could create in the mind of a young Frenchman who is now looked on, as the very reason the WTC became a success.

Petit had only his goal in mind and had grown to see these towers as his most gleaming moment in time and purpose. Petit wanted to tightrope walk across the expanse between the towers. Even more, he wanted to defy death and dance on a rope 110 stories in the sky. So for this little known expert wirewalker, his dream possessed him. So much so, that he came to America and planned for eight years how he would do this dangerous task his heart demanded of him.

Petit said later that these twin towers were like two big dreams, larger than life, that were calling him to do this fearful task. Finally the day came. After posing as a writer for a magazine to gain access to the building and working with a team for several years, he ascended the south tower while another team ascended the other.

Having narrowly passing by security as deliverymen they reached the top and set up the equipment to string the wire across the expanse. With all New York and the World looking on, he moved onto the wire and began a dance higher than any man had ever danced the wire before. One police officer said that when he arrived, he thought to himself that he was seeing a once in a lifetime event that would never be duplicated again. Petit said that when he saw the police officers he laughed, knowing that they had joined the audience and could do nothing to stop this dream come true. Petit lay down on the wire, jumped and danced, and after seeing a bird flying above him 30 to 45 minutes into this amazing act, got up and came to the edge where he was grabbed and arrested. Latter all the charges were dropped and he served community service by performing for children in Central Park.

What Petit had done was greater than just fulfilled his dream, he had made the Twin Towers an amazing point of interest for all New Yorkers. The news media coverage and thousands of watchers from below had made both the towers and Petit a piece of history and folklore of the City that loves a Broadway show. Like a great song in a Musical, New Yorkers began to sing the praise of the heart stopping man on a wire. Another thing started that day eight or nine years ago with Petit's dream. The struggling Twins became hot property and filled up the vacancies. Windows on the World Restaurant opened and the property began to pay for itself, rising from a past of millions in debt.

People began to affectionately show pride for the World Trade Center and from all over the world governments and businesses sought after workspace in the massive highest buildings in New York.[2]

Even against all the odds, many like petit, have had Dreams that lead them to the fame that comes with reaching the goal. Like many dreams, the success doesn't just bring the winning goal, but the benefit of those around who share the glowing results in the community at large.

One of my favorite lines is from a Carley Simon song I know as New Jerusalem. Those words are etched in my mind with every dream I strive for and every goal at hand: " Let The Dreamers Wake The Nation". For only with dreams can any society grow and flourish into a mutual prosperity.

As a young man in college I went to my Physics teacher and asked him about travel at the speed of light, He said: "That would be impossible because energy if burned at the speed of light and the gravity effect would crush you at that speed". I replied: "Why not use attraction instead of propulsion and create your own gravity like the earth does?" Only recently have I noticed searching through patents with the US patent office that someone has applied for a magnetic drive propulsion engine that shows promise of creating a gravity effect that may take man into a new era of near light speed travel.

When you dream big, and think big, you create large tasks beyond the scope of the known into the realm of possibilities. President Kennedy did that for this nation by the dream of a man on the moon. Martian Luther King did it with his dream of racial harmony and love. Ronald Regan did it by inspiring the nation to overcome big government with new ways of thinking about the economy.

---

[2] 2 Petit later published a book, To Reach the Clouds: My High Wire Walk Between the Twin Towers, North Point Press; 1st edition (September 4, 2002) describing his stunt. (Used By Permission: Copyrigth.Com). A Caldecott-award winning children's book called The Man Who Walked Between The Towers, Roaring Brook (July 18, 2003) was written after the September 11, 2001, terrorist act that brought the Twin Towers to the ground. This story is documented in the Biography & Discovery Channel's broadcast 8-23-2003, PBS version found at PBS.ORG "The Center of The World" documentary C 2003 Steeplechase Films and WGBH Educational Foundation. All Rights Reserved.

In the 1980 I attended an Amway convention in Charlotte North Carolina under the Dexter Yeager branch of the Amway opportunity. The convention hall rose a deafening sound of applauds when Ronald Reagan came to the stage to give words of encouragement and speak about the problems with big government and how the democratic party had to be defeated to bring reform. That grass roots effort and the inspiration given by our future president that day was amazing to see first hand. This was early in his campaign and he may have been preaching to the choirs but he still excited an encouraged the audience in such a charismatic way that when I left that convention hall that evening, there was no doubt in my mind that he would be our next president.

Being able to expect greatness and project that positive outcome in such a way is a gift from God and Ronald Regan was not only the great communicator, he was the great inspirational motivator who made you feel like he had personally taken you under his arm and asked you to help him win for the benefit of us all. Someone else who has this great quality that comes hand in hand with his attitude of gratitude is Arnold. If they ever would amend the constitution for someone to run for president, for Arnold they will certainly do it. He ability to unite the polar sides of issues in America today is expert in execution and form. His rise to Governor of California is a good example of how he is able to overcome negative images ascribed to him by his critics and set goals that can benefit both sides of the political isle.

President Kennedy and President Regan had the same quality that attracted the people to support them. When one of these great men walked into the room you knew that they were there. They paid attention to their image and made you feel like you were a part of what they were doing. The room was full of the air of gratitude for what you had helped them to achieve in an expectant way that seemed to speak in the heart that destiny compelled you to vote for them. As a young boy in Cleveland Ohio I remember seeing President Kenney at a democratic political rally on TV. You could feel the energy in the air and the excitement of those there about this great man.

In my mind the greatest Presidents this nation has had are many and a few stand out. George Washington for his prayerful nature and ability to let God grant him miracles. One of my favorite stories of President Washington is told best by the Pennsylvania Indians who recounted how they had shoot at him hundreds of times and could not kill him. They finally gave up and said that 'he was chosen by the Great Spirit'. If you ever come to southwestern Pennsylvania you can visit the fort where he commanded as a young officer and hear the story for yourself.

Another was Abraham Lincoln. There was no greater a defining moment in his career than the Gettysburg address. President Kennedy had an equally defining moment when he became one of the first presidents to set a national goal that seemed beyond our dreams by putting a man on the moon. His inauguration speech is one of the greatest speeches in American history. President Regan also had a defining moment in oratory history when he called for the wall of Berlin to come down. As a republican myself, one might find this statement odd but one of the by far greatest public speakers of today is President Bill Clinton. His ability to argue his point is expert and his charismatic abilities will no doubt bring him into new roles in world history.

What I am getting at is something I learned from a seminar promoter a few years ago. He said that you have to command a performance when you walk into a room. Leadership is like a badge that says I am here and you want to be around me. It is somewhat arrogant yet humble. With an attitude of gratitude for the station in life you achieve and caring for your fellow mankind, you can hone your presence in a room to be motivating and friendly to all who meet you.

Sharing time with your friends and those who seek your advice is a way to give back some of what God has blessed you with and give a helping hand up to a higher station is life.
Your dreams should always be larger and larger with each goal you set. You will set the pace that others will follow if you believe in your efforts and cause. A book I bought as a young man entitled 'The Magic of Thinking Big' should be on your reading list often. I

have a collection of books that help me self motivate and plan bigger ideas and goals each day.

When a famous singer comes on the stage what are you looking for if you're in the audience. The biggest, loudest, most exciting show you ever spent your money on, isn't that right? I know I am. Actors and singers seem to know how to live large and stay busy with new ideas and concepts. I don't agree with her politics yet still I love to hear Barbra Streisand perform. She has a voice that is larger than life and her musical performances are immortal. I love her even though I don't agree with her left views. She knows how to live large. We can all learn something from great people like presidents and performers on how to present our lives in public.

Taking an acting class or singing class can help you to learn how to be a public presence. Public speaking classes and hiring a couch to help you through the newness of the feeling of stage freight is wise to do. That feeling of 'what do I do now that I am about to go on TV', as a corporate President, or what ever your choice in life and business has lead you to, butterflies will be easily dispelled with a little help form those who have been there before.

Enjoy the benefits of what you have accomplished. Go on a vacation once you reach different levels in your goals and plans. Spend time with your family and don't let the years go by before you have taken the time to play with your children.

Once you reach your monetary goals, you will set your own schedule, be your own boss, and you will get there by Dreaming big, thinking big, and then you live large.

Summary and Recommended Reading

The fourteen rules that I used to gain wealth are listed below. They are not hard and fast rules, rather concepts by which one can achieve wealth. They are:

1. Always a borrower and a lender be

2. Sale at a profit of 300% mark up

3. Thoughts and Ideas are worth millions

4. Real Estate, Real Estate, Real Estate

5. Savings are the start of all transactions

6. Never seek money above Love or others

7. Poverty is a mental condition

8. Millionaires visualize their dreams

9. $100 bills cost the mint 6.5 cents

10. Give and it shall be given unto you

11. Dress the part, lead with your heart

12. True success is not measured in money

13. You can't take it with you

14. Dream Big, Think Big, Live Large

Along with retraining your mind to succeed you will need to understand that the reason we are where we are today is because we continue to do the same things, which are familiar to us. If we continue to do the things we've done, we'll continue to get what we've got.

I sure you have heard of Maslow and his pyramid of self-actualization. This psychologist came up with a good way to show how we achieve our station in life and how we lean and grow into a comfortable set of feelings about ourselves.

Pavlov was another psychologist who showed that we could be programmed to respond to the same events in the same way, even when the situation has changed.
To prove this he took dogs and measured their saliva output when he rang a bell and then feed them on a regular time schedule. After a long period of time doing the same thing, ringing the bell, he then changed the event and didn't feed the dogs at the bell. The dogs still started to salivate at the sound of the bell even thought the situation had changed and there was no food.

This book is a way to program your thinking into a new opinion of yourself as an entrepreneur and successful millionaire. On the way you may want to read what I have read in the past that has helped me to achieve what I have.

Remember when earlier in this book we talked about learning how to achieve wealth in life. The best way to learn how to be a billionaire is to go learn from one. He did it and can show you what is required to achieve that level. In my opinion it is the same with a multi-millionaires and billionaires. The best teachers are the ones who have worked at that profession. That is why the SBA has retired business owners who will help you in their programs.
Ken Gaub writes in his book that goals are like a road map. You don't know where your going until you know how to get there. Goals are like looking at that map and saying before you drive, this is the best road to take. Seek out experts on your road and ask for help. Mentors are important to any person who is on the road to millionaire status.

Decide at what point you are going to retire. Insure that you choose time periods to rest on a regular bases so that you can enjoy the benefits of your success and your family. Making memories together are like the MasterCard commercial, priceless.

When attending a sales training in Cleveland a man gave me a book entitled Welfare A Novocain. He was a middle age African American man dressed in a suit and tie and so, I talked with him a while. He shared with me how he knew many people on welfare that didn't really need it. He told me how he had worked all his life and never asked for a hand out from anybody. He was very proud of that fact. Later on I did some research on the Welfare system. When I checked on the stats, there were nearly twice as many whites on the welfare rolls as there were blacks. The African American community in this country is full of hard working people who have in the past gotten a bad rap. This man was showing his efforts to overcome the negative image that many had portrayed in racist ways when I was a child. His premise was very true, welfare is exactly like Novocain and the system is the Novocain, the temporary pain is gone but the problem is still there.

Poverty is a mentality and it has affected all races, creeds, and nationalities, even some Republicans. To combat the mental conditioning we need to reprogram our expectations by placing goal oriented visualizations throughout our life. Placing pictures of what we will achieve and placing target dates on the photos will help to let our mind see where we are headed.

It only takes $650 to print a million dollars worth of one hundred dollar bills. Knowing that money is a game with rules will help us to learn how to play to win. Since the US Treasury prints more money all the time your winning at the game does not mean that others have to lose.
Real Estate is one of the fastest ways to get rich slow and provides a regular monthly income. Building a real estate portfolio of many units to build on will help you increase your net worth and give you an appreciating asset that has progressively gone up even in down stock markets.

Giving to others is a way to benefit the community of mankind at large and is worth more in the benefits you receive than the cost of the gift. God rewards us for our benevolence to others less fortunate and as the preacher said, you can never out give God.

Dressing for success is like putting on a costume for a play in which you are about to perform. Like a star in a movie you must act your part from your heart so that the audience will believe that you are really the person you portray to them. To be believed in this role you must first believe it yourself.

True wealth is not measured in material wealth or money but in what you leave behind in intangible value you brought to others lives. Perhaps you are not going to be a millionaire in businesses. You may fit into Gods plan as a soul winner of millions for Christ. You may become the doctor that will find the cure for AIDS. Perhaps you are the leader that will bring peace to warring factions in Africa.

The concepts in this book will help you to learn that there is no such thing as failure, only learning experiences from which you correct mistakes. Every set back is a small battle from which the lessons help to win the war.

The only way to truly fail is to never really try. If you are an awful singer, you may still be a great comedian. Find your talent in Gods plan and do it.

We all have talent at doing something or we can learn how from those who did.

Your goals and plans should be ever larger with each new achievement. Always plan five years ahead and plan to leave behind a legacy for your heirs.

Remember that you will take nothing to the grave with you but you. All your wealth will transfer in ownership to those who you are responsible to God for blessing. They in turn, will leave it behind to others. If you plan right you will create generational wealth with which your future generations can do great things in your name and proxy.

Proper planning in a will and in trusts, foundations and corporations, can help you improve the standard of living in the community and your families life long after you are gone.

Employing workers in America as your company grows helps to stimulate the economy and helps to place you in key strategic locations in the cycle of money flow. Generating a positive team environment around you will help others to feel self actualized in helping you reach your goals and make your employees proud to be part of a winning company.

Follow the rules and pay your taxes when due and contribute to the safety net for those who honestly cannot work. Offer a helping hand to others who are seeking a way out of the system that has them enslaved in low wage jobs and nonproductive behavior.

I believe that there will be a judgment day. On that day we will not be measured in what we did. We will be measured in how much faith we had and how we put that faith into action for Gods will and the benefit of others. When we dream build and grow wealth using our talents as God has given to us, we benefit others more than ourselves and reap the rewards of blessings for our families.

Knowing where you have come from is beneficial to help you understand where you are going. Obeying the Ten Commandments even if your not Jewish is not just beneficial for a blessing in most cases it is the law. Thou shalt not steal, kill, and other forms of cheating are rules that governments and lawmakers have set up to keep the playing field even for all.

Creative ideas and big thinking is worth millions when coupled with actions to complete the goal. As this country moves toward an investor-based economy, we should all learn to cooperate with the tasks set before us to help the uneducated learn how to become successful.

Millionaires are not born that way all the time. Very few are born into wealth. Sales and being a millionaire is a learned profession just like doctors and lawyers or any other profession in life.

Here are lists of resources that are my recommended reading. As you build your business, you will want to purchase these fine authors books, tapes, and courses to help you learn the profession of independently wealthy self made millionaire. This list is also where I got my ideas. I just changed some of the wording to express it in my own terms and share my own experiences.

RECCOMENDED READING:
Dreams, Plans, Goals; Ken Gaub
No Down Payment; Carleton Sheets
Rich Dad, Poor Dad; Robert Kiyosaki
Secrets of Closing The Sale; Zig Ziglar
How To Master The Art of Selling; Tom Hopkins
Trump The Art of The Deal; Donald Trump
How To Win Friends And Influence People; Dale Carnegie
The Power of Positive Thinking; Norman Vincent Peal
Think and Grow Rich; Napoleon Hill
The Magic of Thinking Big; David Schwartz
The Go Getter; Peter B. Kyne

Here is a list of companies that offer employment in the field of selling that will lead to becoming a self made millionaire when you faithfully follow their training programs and directions. What you can learn here is psychology and technique. What you do with this information is up to you.

OPPORTUNITY LIST:
RDJ Catalog, Inc.; www.rdjcatalog.com;
www.InstructionsToMoney.com
Professional Education Institute; **www.carletonsheets.com**
Scott Fetzer Kirby Company; **www.kirby.com**
Health-mor Inc. (HMI Industries); **www.filterqueen.com**
Cutco/Vector; **www.cutco.com**
        www.workforstudents.com
        www.earnparttime.com

It is important to track how you are doing and see how far you have to go to reach your goal. The only report card that matters in the world of money is a net worth statement. Here is an example of a net worth statement:

Assets	Description	Market or Appraised Value
Real Estate	12 rental properties	$678.900.00
Stocks & Bonds	E*Trade Financial	$58,900.00
Collectable Coins	Bullion & US 1700-2005	$1,580,000
Business Equipment	Furniture & Fixtures	$79,000.00
Art & Antiques	Paintings / Historical	$50,000.00
Household Furnishings	Appliance / Decor	$30,500.00
Tools & Equipment	Woodworking/ Mechanic	$20,000.00
Autos	2004 Ford / 1999 Chevy	$35,800.00
TOTAL ASSETS	**Gross Worth**	**$2,538,100.00**
Liabilities		( )denotes negative number
Mortgages	Rental Property	($400,000.00)
Credit Card Debt	Visa/MasterCard/Store	($50,000.00)
Auto Loans	2004 Ford / 1999 Chevy	($18,000.00)
SBA Business loan	My Retail Store	($30,000.00)
TOTAL LIABILITIES	**Gross Debt**	**($498,000.00)**
NET WORTH		**$2,040,100.00**

Doing a net worth statement will help you identify areas to work on and help you to see the hidden value locked in your attic as well. Get granddad's old pocket watch out and get in appraised. Include in your net worth statement your own home, jewelry, inventory, and everything that you own. You should do a net worth statement every month. Bankers use your net worth statement to determine your financial health when reviewing your application for a loan. When you fill out the loan form a net worth format is built into the form. So it is important to have one ready to transfer the information when buying real estate.

Carleton Sheets web site has a great financial freedom planner that will help you to do this on computer. I recommend this program and his real estate tool kit.

Having Quicken or MS Money programs will help also. Keeping track of your credit and financial health is a wise and easy thing to do with a computer.

If you are starting out with bad credit, as I was in the beginning, you will want to get a copy of your credit report and contact your debtors. Make arrangements to begin paying something every month until the debt is paid. In three to five years you will be surprised how your credit will improve. Even if you do not have bad credit, use your credit only for things you need to help you make money.

In economics classes worldwide they teach the Guns and Butter analogy. With guns you can get all the butter you want. So invest first in money producing efforts with your credit and you will soon be able to enjoy lots of butter.

I have tried in this book to give you a starting point to begin a new understanding of how to acquire wealth. It is by no means all the answers. As you grow and learn to find new sources of information, pass it on to your fiends and family.
Word of mouth is still the best form of advertising in the world. You will be surprised how much business you get in what ever you do in life from word of mouth. Many of my rental units have been rented because someone was talking about my successes and told them to call me when they were looking for a place to rent.

The Internet has made it a whole lot easier to get information, buy and look at real estate on the net, and just get things done. As a young man we had to search the old fashion way at the library. The library is still a good source of information that is not on the net in many books and archives. I try to spend at least two to three hours a month at the library. One of the great things about the library is that you can borrow a book to read first and see if you want to add it to your library by purchasing it later. If you are on welfare and buying a book is totally out of the question now, the library is the place to get started.

I hope that the contents of this book have not offended you. I am a republican and a believer in God. You do not have to agree with me to acquire wealth. Using my methods and resources will benefit your life in any endeavor you choose regardless of your political or religious affiliation. I do hope that you will see the logic in my arguments for a more conservative approach to finances and business being a means to be as benevolent every liberal would desire. The true compassionate does something to change things in the face of injustice.

Actions speak louder than words do every day 24,7,365 and 366 on leap year.

Give your self a chance to make mistakes but do the study first. Find experts and learn from them. In my own experience in 1992 I was living in a trailer on about $700.00 including food stamps. The system is designed to provide a safety net that I am proud to pay taxes and support. Today I live in a wonderful home valued over one hundred thousand. I have want of nothing other than to continue success to insure my children are well provided for. I thank God that he has given my Wife and I the ability in this great country to bring our family together in an effort to achieve what we have. I can do nothing in life alone. Building a network of family, friends, partners, mentors and allies will help you too.

I could not close this book without writing some words about security. When you start to make money the spoof emails and con men will try anything to get it. In fact, even when you don't have much money they try. Here are some rules that you should use to avoid problems with con men.

Never answer an email that is from a credit card company, bank, or any other email that asks for account information. This includes the ones from Nigeria that say they are some rich mans son and they need your bank account number to get 50,000,000 out of their country. No body is going to give you something for nothing. They may call on the phone also thinking you are dumb and say someone stole your credit card number and they need to verify it to see if its yours.

Never give out personal information like your social security number unless you have called the person who you are giving it to. Then only do it when it is absolutely necessary like with the Social Security Department. If someone is calling you from your bank, credit card Company, or Social Security, they will already have your numbers including the security code on the signature line on the back of the card. It is in their system. Giving out bank or credit card numbers on the Internet through emails is not smart. The cons will bleed your account dry and move to new offices in the blink of an eye. Many of these cons are not even in this country. That means they are out of reach for our law enforcement.

Valid secure websites have encrypted certificates and your credit card information is never emailed anywhere in most cases. If it is, then it is encrypted with 128 bit or higher settings so that no one who is not authorized to process your order and get your payment for your order to the right place ever sees it.

On our web site RDJ Catalog.Com, we never see your credit card numbers. It goes right to the banks server and we only see a report that includes your shipping address, name, email, phone, and the last four numbers of the credit card you used. We have SSL encryption that ensures that our customers are safe when buying on line with us.

Put code words on your credit card. The Mothers Maiden name thing is easy for a skilled con to get. There are ways that they can access your family history and find out what your or your mother's maiden name is to.

Lot of items are public record so make up a word totally unrelated to you and where you live and ask your credit card company to request the security words before allowing phone access to your accounts. Citi cards calls me and asks if a charge on the card made at this location at this time was me to check for fraud. I gave them my cell phone so if I am not at home they can contact me and check before charging a large purchase. They never ask for information of any kind, they just verify the charge.

When keeping important papers at home, keep them in a fire safe. Credit cards and other documents when not in use are best kept in a home safe so that if someone gets their nose where it doesn't belong you can guard against temptation.

Buy a shredder and do not throw out old credit card bills, bank statements, or letters with personal information. I shred all my mail when I am done with it including credit card offers to insure that someone else isn't applying in my name.

Get a home security system. Brinks and AMD are among the few who offer home protection systems and they are less expensive than a break in or lose of life. Many have built in fire and carbon monoxide systems also that can insure that you and your family are safe in an emergency.

Face the truth that we are all con artist targets and subject to their techniques. Expert cons are able to manipulate anyone. Don't think that you're bulletproof. There is a way to safe guard when doing deals. Ask for a background check and valid ID search. Get a police report release and pay for a known felon report. Never give money in cash for any large deal. Always us a check and insure that the person you are paying has the goods at closing. Use an escrow account to close deals and have written agreements on the quality of goods exchanged or performance requirements of the seller.

With real estate always get title insurance. Use a lawyer to complete all transactions. If the deal is so good, it will be their tomorrow. Don't allow your self to be pressured into a large purchase to fast. With some direct sales purchases like a Kirby or Cookware, if the purchase is in your home, there is a minimum three days cancellation period in my state. In some it is ten or fifteen business days not including weekends or holidays. Insure that you have done all you can to protect your assets from being stolen and you will have less chances of being ripped off.

I have not begun to cover everything that needs to be covered in a book about this subject. I have honestly tried with every word to inform you of how I did it.
Money is not the ends, it is the means. So if you try and fail, try again. Don't ever give up.

If your goal in reading this book is to learn how to make money to start a ministry or mission, then you should also be aware of the opportunities out there with grant organizations. Many non-profit organizations have money to give, but you have got to meet their standards. These organizations do not give it away for personal use unless it is for a Doctor to go on medical missions and cover travel expenses or something like that. A search on the Internet will give you a good start. Check with your pastor, rabbi, or clergy in the local community and they will direct you toward your goal if it is service to others.

I feel that once you can afford it, everyone should do a year of service in some area. Even if it isn't a Peace Corp overseas mission, there are places here in the USA that needs volunteers like you. I was a volunteer in the Army and learned more in my time in service about the world than all my years in schooling.

Now you are ready to begin your road to success. Start by writing your goals down and what you're going to do with the money. Money it self is not a goal in itself. To achieve you must have a reward at the end to make it motivational.

Here is my goal for this book, sell one million copies in two years or less. What will I do with the money: Buy a 100 plus unit real estate property & Help a missionary in Central America. Take my family to Disney Land in California. Take my wife to Hawaii. (Notice I didn't say the kid's honey).

God made you and he designed you for success, my prayers are with you as you begin your journey with the instructions to money. When you gain success, write me and let me know how this book has helped you. I enjoy reading letters from readers of my work and will be glad to get your feedback.

My purpose in this book was not to give you all the answers. My purpose was to give you some of the insight and knowledge that I gained along the way. A wise man once told me that wisdom is knowledge in action. Life should be a continuing learning experience. Putting what we learn in life into action is the responsibility we are tasked with by life. The true rewards are not in the things we own. The true rewards are in the people we touch and help along the way..

What's Happening To Money

It is now 2010 and what has happened as a result of writing this book in 2006 has been awesome. After Instructions To Money first came out, I started a syndicated radio show which can be found on the web at www.InstructionsToMoney.com

On the show over the years I have interviewed some of the best known experts on finance, business start-ups, and money. Authors like Carleton Sheets, Robert Kiyosaki and his wife Kim, and countless others who have expertise in investing and wealth management.

I also was invited with my family to the White House to meet President Bush. That was one of the greatest days of my life.

Recently we expanded our small company and added a Public Relations service at www.VIPPR.org The company has centered on Christian and Family Friendly clients for the most part. We have had countless book signings, TV, Radio and media appearances. Just recently I appeared on TCT TV show *"I'm Just Sayin"* with Pastor Dan Willis.

Over the last few years, people have asked me what is happening to money and if my ideas are still applicable today. The ideas and principles in this book are still sound in building a business and changing your attitude for success in life. As for what is happening to money, the answer is found on the front page news and in a 2000 year old Bible prophesies.

Money has lost its value by over printing to pay for the bailout bills. Money in the world of computers and banking is no more than electronic credits. Higher costs for printing is making governments world wide go to cashless transactions to pay for debts like Social Security, Veterans Pensions, and even programs like food stamps.

Bible Prophets foretold of a cashless society. (Rev. Ch. 13)

Revelation 13:15-18 *And he had power to give life unto the image of the beast, that the image of the beast should both speak, and cause that as many as would not worship the image of the beast should be killed. And he causeth all, both small and great, rich and poor, free and bond, to receive a mark in their right hand, or in their foreheads: And that no man might buy or sell, save he that had the mark, or the name of the beast, or the number of his name. Here is wisdom. Let him that hath understanding count the number of the beast: for it is the number of a man; and his number is Six hundred threescore and six.*

(King James 1634 Version)

right[G1188] hand,[G5495] Literally means in the Greek Right Side of the Body. (Strong's Concordance)

G1188 δεξιός dexios   *dex-ee-os'*   From [G1209]; the *right* side or (feminine) hand (as that which usually *takes*): - right (hand, side).

G1909 ἐπί epi   *ep-ee'*

A primary preposition properly meaning *superimposition* (of time, place, order, etc.), as a relation of *distribution* [with the genitive case], that is, *over, upon,* etc.; of *rest* (with the dative case) *at, on,* etc.; of *direction* (with the accusative case) *towards, upon,* etc.: - about (the times), above, after, against, among, as long as (touching), at, beside, X have charge of, (be-, [where-]) fore, in (a place, as much as, the time of, -to), (because) of, (up-) on (behalf of) over, (by, for) the space of, through (-out), (un-) to (-ward), with. In compounds it retains essentially the same import, *at, upon,* etc. (literally or figuratively).

Reference: Strong's Concordance (The "G" stands for Greek and the number is a reference word numbering system for the words in the Bible).

A mark[G5480] in[G1909] Literally means in the Greek a Etching or Cutting into or under the skin.

If you have not been by the Alex Jones sites online or the anti-NOW (New World order) groups then you may want to fasten your seat belt and get your prayer rug out for this one.

This 2000 year old prophesy is coming true very soon. The Cashless society is now here with the Verichip implant and the Halochip ID systems. Corporations like SteelVault and Verichip have announced a merger that along with IBM will be able to track persons via GPS (Global Position Satellite) and lojack the human body with a computer chip. The new systems are designed to work with a 16 to 18 digit number ID embedded inside the chip along with Banking, Finance, Medical, and Credit records.

The Cashless Society:

Verichip Corporation has made the microchip (Invented by Dr. Daniel Mann) a implantable device approved by the FDA for the following use:

Medical Records ~ GPS Tracking ~ Identification ~ Cashless Transactions

Recent merger with Steel Vault Corporation and new agreements with IBM who is doing the census on US Government contract, gives the new rice sized Verichip all the qualities that the Mark of the Beast would require.

A close inspection of Verimed web site shows the uniform method for implanting these chips into people is right in line with Bible Prophesy:

For Doctors to have a standard location to collect the RFID (radio frequency identification) that connects computer readers to the information, Verichip policy is to require all implanted chips be put **into the right arm or forehead** for double amputees.

The new Health Care Bill just passed by Congress under the Obama Administration has provisions in it for a computer chip ID implant and other bio-medical implants included in the law. This will make it possible for the government to attach all your bank accounts, medical records, and charge you via EFT (Electronic Funds Transfer) for any co-pay or costs associated with socialist health care.

It is obvious that the Biblical prophets words have come true and that the 'Mark of the Beast' as it has been called, is here at our door step.

With projected debts and hyperinflation I have some investments in gold and silver to offset the event of the cashless implant law and take a stand against the forced 'chipping' of we the people. Obama's communist agenda may not just be a political and ideological shift in world policy in governments, it may also be what I call prophesy in motion. These things are the design of an end-time scenario right out of the pages of the Bible. A real life "Left Behind" saga is unfolding in the world today and the wise person is cautioned by spiritual intuition to prepare for eternity.

"What does it profit a man if he gains the whole world and losses his soul"?
(The Bible)

Money in paper and coin will soon go the way of the button hook and other outdated systems. In today's computer age we are seeing the coming of the cashless transaction where wallets, credit cards, and money are all in the right hand or forehead as the Bible foretold.

I recommend that if you have not prayed and accepted Yahshua Messiah (Jesus Christ) as your saviour, there is no better time than right now. According to the Bible, all those who receive this "Mark" inside the right hand or forehead will be thrown into the lake of fire, which is called the second death. (Rev. Ch. 19 – 21)

Even Hell and Death are thrown into this "Lake of Fire" along with the Devil and his demons. On Judgment Day the important thing is not how much you made in money, but what you did with it to help others and lead people to salvation from the Lake of Fire.

Please feel free to visit our web sites and read more on faith in Messiah at
www.ThinkYah.org and www.YahsWayTV.org In the fall 2010 we will begin airing a TV show about the Messianic Jewish faith and we invite you to stop by and watch us on TCT TV world wide.

You can also get copies of the other books I have written at these web sites and gain insight into the relationship with messiah that I hold to and the faith that defies religion and worships Yahweh God in Spirit and in Truth.

If you have any Questions you can contact me via email at my web sites or write me at; 858 Route 446 Smethport, PA 16749.

As I said before, the true rewards are in the people we touch and help along the way.
May God bless you to have the diamonds of gratitude from those you touch, the gold of happiness, and an excessive net worth of love in your bank vault in heaven. I hope that this book will help you in starting that investment program today. Finally, always remember, money doesn't grow on trees, it grows in brains. The Greatest Reward is Eternal life through Yahshua Messiah.

Bibliography: See my reading list of recommended books at www.RDJCatalog.Com and www.InstructionsToMoney.Com

Title: How To Master The Art of Selling **By:** Tom Hopkins **Paperback:** 292 pages **Publisher:** Warner Books; Reissue edition (October 20, 1988) **ISBN:** 0446386367

Title: Secrets of Closing The Sale **By:** Zig Ziglar **Paperback:** 410 pages **Publisher:** Berkley Publishing Group; Reissue edition (August 1985) **ISBN:** 0425081028

Title: World's Greatest Wealth Builder **By:** Carleton Sheets **Paperback:** 313 pages **Publisher:** Bonus Books (October 25, 1998) **ISBN:** 1566251117

Title: No Down Payment **By:** Carleton Sheets **Course Publisher:** The Professional Education Institute © 2006 Carleton H. Sheets. Can Order From: RDJCATALOG.COM

Title: Dreams Plans Goals **By:** Ken Gaub **Paperback:** 144 pages **Publisher:** New Leaf Press (July 1993) **ISBN:** 0892212446

Title: Think & Grow Rich **By:** Napoleon Hill **Paperback:** 254 pages **Publisher:** Ballantine Books; Reissue edition (May 12, 1987) **ISBN:** 0449214923

Title: How to Win Friends & Influence People **By:** Dale Carnegie **Paperback:** 264 pages **Publisher:** Pocket; Reissue edition (February 15, 1990) **ISBN:** 0671723650

Title: TRUMP The Art Of The Deal **By:** Donald J. Trump with Tony Schwartz **Paperback:** 372 pages **Publisher:** Warner Books; Reprint edition (January 1, 1989)   **ISBN:** 0446353256

Title: The Go-Getter **By:** Peter B. Kyne **Paperback:** 68 pages **Publisher:** Standard Publications, Inc. (December 2005) **ISBN:** 1594621039

Title: Welfare: A Novocain **By:** Lateef Muhammad **Paperback:** 75 pages **Publisher:** Designer Communications. (1991) **ISBN:** 0962766313

Title: The Magic Of Thinking Big **By:** Dr. David J. Schwartz **Paperback:** 192 pages **Publisher:** Fireside; Reprint edition (April 2, 1987) **ISBN:** 0671646788

Title: To Reach the Clouds: My High Wire Walk Between the Twin Towers **By:** Philippe Petit **Hardcover:** 256 pages **Publisher:** North Point Press; 1st edition (September 4, 2002) **ISBN:** 0865476519

Twin Towers story is documented in the Biography & Discovery Channel's broadcast 8-23-2003, <u>PBS version found at PBS.ORG</u> ,*"The Center of The World"* documentary © 2003 Steeplechase Films and WGBH Educational Foundation. (Used by Permission)

www.RDJCatalog.Com

www.PRSpaceBook.Com

www.InstructionsToMoney.Com

www.YahsWayTV.Org